Contents

Happiness

A to Z

Evidence-Based Strategies for Achieving Well-being and Fulfilment

Dr. Badri Bajaj

Happiness A-Z:
Evidence-based strategies for achieving well-being and fulfilment

© Pavilion Publishing & Media

The author has asserted his rights in accordance with the Copyright, Designs and Patents Act (1988) to be identified as the author of this work.

Published by:
Pavilion Publishing and Media Ltd
Blue Sky Offices, 25 Cecil Pashley Way, Shoreham by Sea, West Sussex, BN43 5FF

Tel: +44 (0)1273 434943
Email: info@pavpub.com
Web: www.pavpub.com

Published 2025

A catalogue record for this book is available from the British Library.

ISBN: 978-1-80388-439-4

Pavilion Publishing and Media is a leading publisher of books, training materials and digital content in mental health, social care and allied fields. Pavilion and its imprints offer must-have knowledge and innovative learning solutions underpinned by sound research and professional values.

Cover design: Emma Dawe
Page layout and typesetting: Phil Morash
Printing: CPI Group (UK) Ltd

About the author

Dr. Badri Bajaj is a global thought leader and practitioner in coaching, well-being, and leadership. He is an Associate Professor at Jaypee Institute of Information Technology, Noida, India, and has published extensively on coaching, mindfulness, leadership, well-being, and emotional intelligence. In 2017, he was honoured with the *100 Best Global Coaching Leaders Award* by CHRO Asia and the World HRD Congress.

Dr. Bajaj has trained and coached leaders across IT, retail, the Indian Navy, and professional associations, delivering talks in India, the UK, and the USA. As former President of the ICF Delhi Chapter, he spearheaded impactful initiatives and secured prestigious awards for the chapter. His work bridges research and practice to advance both personal and organizational well-being.

Dedicated to my family and mentors

Acknowledgements

Writing *Happiness A-Z* has been a journey of reflection, learning and gratitude. This book would not have been possible without the support, wisdom and inspiration of many individuals who have contributed to my understanding of happiness and well-being.

First and foremost, I extend my heartfelt gratitude to my family, whose love, encouragement and unwavering belief in me have been a constant source of strength. Your presence brings joy and meaning to my life every day.

I am deeply thankful to my mentors, colleagues and friends who have enriched my journey with their insights and thoughtful conversations. Your perspectives have shaped my thinking, and your support has been invaluable.

A special note of appreciation to the experts and thought leaders whose wisdom has guided my exploration of happiness. Your research, ideas and reflections have provided a strong foundation for this book, and I am grateful for the opportunity to learn from your work.

I also extend my sincere thanks to the many individuals who generously shared their true stories for different chapters of this book. Your openness and experiences bring depth and authenticity to these pages, making happiness not just an abstract concept but a lived reality. Your stories serve as powerful reminders of resilience, gratitude and the diverse paths that lead to a fulfilling life.

My grateful thanks to Archishree Gupta for contributing the illustrations for this book.

A sincere thank you to my students, whose curiosity and eagerness to learn continually inspire me. Your questions and reflections have challenged me to think more deeply and explore happiness from multiple dimensions.

My gratitude also goes to my publishers, editors and everyone involved in bringing this book to life. Your dedication and expertise have helped refine and present these ideas in a way that I hope will resonate with readers.

Finally, to my readers – thank you for embarking on this journey with me. May this book serve as a guide, and a reminder that happiness is not just a destination but a way of living. May you find joy, meaning and fulfilment in the small moments and the grand experiences of life.

With gratitude,
Dr Badri Bajaj

List of individuals who contributed stories:

Birgitte Ekström, Sweden.
Psychotherapist and coach.

Iain McCormick, New Zealand.
Coach, author and coach trainer.

Tim Anstiss, UK.
Medical doctor and coach trainer.

Rajiv Naithani, India.
SVP – HR & OD, Persistent Systems.

Andrea Giraldez-Hayes, UK.
Coaching psychologist, psychotherapist and consultant.

Aitana Leret, France.
Professional coach unlocking leadership from within.

Jonathan Passmore, UK.
Professor, Henley Business School and SVP, EZRA.

Marcia Reynolds, USA.
Committed to transforming minds and hearts through coaching.

Fabiana Memmolo, USA.
Positive psychology coach and researcher.

Mongezi C Makhalima, South Africa.
Thinkers 50 Global Coach.

Ian Day, UK.
Centre for Lifelong Learning, University of Warwick.

Holly Andrews, UK.
Henley Business School.

Pamela Larde, USA.
Author, professor, entrepreneur and joy researcher.

Sam Isaacson, UK.
Founder of the Coachtech Collective and co-founder of AIcoach.chat.

Ioanna Iordanou, UK.
Reader in HRM, Oxford Brookes University.

Jane Daly, UK.
Behavioural Scientist, Executive Coach and founder of Peoplestar.

Neal Sundberg, USA.
Director of Coaching at Brightline.

Jolanta Burke, Ireland.
RCSI University of Medicine and Health Sciences.

Gina Phelps Thoebes, USA.
VP Organizational Performance, Arizona Cardinals Football Club.

David Love, UK.
Art-based coach and supervisor, management cartoonist.

Sarah Leach, UK.
Executive coach, educator and author.

Fatima Hussain, India.
Psychologist and researcher specializing in human potential.

Robert Biswas-Diener, USA.
Well-being researcher and author.

Lindsay Oades, Australia.
Professor of Wellbeing Science, University of Melbourne.

David Tee, UK.
Coaching psychologist with a passion for tech possibilities.

Catherine Steele, UK.
Occupational and Coaching Psychologist, University of Leicester.

Stefan Cantore, UK.
University Lecturer, OD Consultant and Executive Coach.

Ana Paula Nacif, UK.
Senior Lecturer, University of East London.

Amit Agnihotri, India.
Founder, MBAUniverse.com and Convenor, IMC.

Ekta Singh, India.
Assistant Professor, Jaypee Institute of Information Technology.

Santoshi Sengupta, India.
Professor, Graphic Era Hill University, Bhimtal.

Introduction

When I came to realize that happiness can be enhanced, I became deeply curious about how to cultivate more of it in my own life. Through exploration and practice, I discovered that happiness is not just a fleeting emotion but something that can be scientifically nurtured and strengthened. This realization inspired me to write *Happiness A-Z*, to share the evidence-backed ways in which anyone can enhance their happiness in simple yet meaningful ways.

Happiness A-Z is designed to be a comprehensive and practical guide to understanding and increasing happiness, presenting twenty-six evidence-based methods. It combines scientific research, expert insights and real-life experiences into an easy-to-follow format. Each chapter explores the method's role in enhancing happiness, the supporting science, practical applications, real-life examples, an engaging activity, and reflective questions to deepen the learning experience.

More than just a book, *Happiness A-Z* is a toolkit for transformation. Its broad scope, motivational tone and adaptable strategies make it a valuable resource for anyone seeking to cultivate greater joy in their own life and the lives of others. The methods are practical, actionable and easy to implement, allowing you to integrate them seamlessly into your daily life. As you turn these pages, you will not just be reading – you will be embarking on a journey to discover your own capacity for happiness.

I encourage you to actively engage with this book. Try the suggested activities, reflect on the exploratory questions, and draw inspiration from the real-life stories shared by remarkable individuals. Let this book be a companion that you revisit at different stages of life, applying its insights in new ways. Most importantly, I invite you to share what you learn with others, spreading happiness beyond yourself and creating ripples of positivity in the world around you.

Chapter 1:

Appreciation

"Appreciate everything, even the ordinary.
Especially the ordinary."

Pema Chödrön

His Holiness the Dalai Lama suggests that we can increase our happiness by reflecting on all the things that we have. The path to inner contentment is not to have what we want, but rather to appreciate what we have. He emphasized that the only way to go through life is to look at our assets and see what we can still do.[1]

---

1   Dalai Lama & Cutler, 1998

Appreciation is the practice of focusing on what we have rather than what we lack. It involves acknowledging the good things in life, whether big or small. By focusing on good things rather than challenges and misfortunes, we develop a positive outlook. Appreciating what we have also helps us adapt to the environment and find fulfilment in the present moment.

Appreciation is acknowledging the value and meaning of something – for instance an event, person, behaviour or object – and feeling a positive emotional connection to it. Appreciation helps us to shift our focus from what may be lacking to abundance and positivity, leading us to acknowledge and appreciate everyday moments and blessings. This acknowledgement encourages us to pursue meaningful goals based on our current resources. We must practice acknowledging the good things in life by reminding ourselves of them, writing about them in a journal, and expressing our feelings about them in front of other people.

One inspiring example of how appreciation transforms life even in the face of profound adversity comes from a cancer survivor's journey. Birgitte Ekström shares:

Next week it will be a year since I was diagnosed with breast cancer. Since then, I have undergone surgery with breast restoration, chemotherapy and radiation, and lastly being pushed into a chemical menopause – all in the name of saving my life and preventing new disease. It is hard to describe the depth of this transformation, but for eight months I only spoke to my nearest family – plus two friends, every other week. I didn't leave my neighbourhood for four months. There simply was no energy for anything but coping.

I heard this chemo-wipe-out described as a 'near death experience', even on a psychological level. To get through the day, I had to let go of most of my identity markers – my way of being a mother, a spouse, a woman, my job as a consultant, my relationships, my dreams, wishes, urges, my body's youth and even my hair colour, when it grew back. There was hardly anything to hang on to in the limbo I found myself in. I couldn't read, watch a thriller ⊠ my mind was foggy, and I couldn't focus and take in anything that would normally nurture me.

In this limbo of free falling, I found a gem. I found freedom, beauty and a deep gratitude for life itself – and a gratitude for the many things I normally take for granted. By letting go of what normally defines me, I discovered that beyond my loved ones, my health, a certain financial stability, nature and my meditations/spirit, I don't need anything from outer life to be deeply happy. It is all right here, when we listen deeply. The purest beauty and joy.

This deep knowing sets me free like never before. Anything that shows up on the outer side of life is a pure bonus for me to enjoy – if I want to. I can say "no", I can say "Yes, please". My life is so rich, and everything is much more precious and joyful than it used to be. I am now in the process of meeting life and finding out who I have become in the process. I undoubtedly feel stronger, wiser and more grounded and enthusiastic than ever before.

Birgitte's story reminds us that practicing appreciation can reveal life's inherent richness, even during the most challenging times, leading to a much deeper sense of joy and fulfilment.

Appreciation may also stem from recognizing the unique blend of nature, culture and opportunity that is present in our surroundings, as beautifully described by Iain McCormick:

Appreciation means the enjoyment of the good things in life, and where I live is one of them. I live in Auckland, New Zealand, the city known as Tāmaki Makaurau in Māori, the language of our thriving one million indigenous people. By international standards, the city of Auckland is small, with just on and a half million people. It is often called the City of Sails because it has several large harbours, favourite spots for people to sail yachts. I greatly appreciate the natural beauty of the volcanic cones, green forests and excellent beaches that surround the city. I walk every day along a wonderful waterfront boardwalk and enjoy the views of the ocean and the volcanic island known as Rangitoto, the youngest and largest volcano in the area which erupted some six hundred years ago.

On my daily walks, I often think that, despite all the beauty, the disadvantage of living on an island in the South Pacific is that it is geographically isolated. It takes more than twenty-four hours to fly from Auckland to London. As an author and executive coach, I need to connect to the wider world if my work is to have the kind of reach and significance that I want. I am hugely grateful to live in the digital age where the tyranny of distance is largely eliminated. I can connect with friends in Europe, give webinars in India and have my books and articles published internationally. Yesterday I did a webinar on Schema Coaching to an audience of over a hundred people in ten countries; that is so exciting. What an experience to generate happiness and appreciation. It is so easy to be so appreciative of all these good things in life.

Iain's heartfelt reflection reminds us to cherish the beauty and opportunities in our lives, fostering a deeper sense of happiness and appreciation for the world around us.

The two stories have very different contexts. Birgitte's focuses on life's inherent richness during the most challenging times, and Iain's on cherishing beauty and opportunities. Birgitte and Iain have created peace and fulfilment in their lives by appreciating what they have. Both their stories inspire us to focus on what we have, rather than dwelling on what we lack.

Appreciation and happiness

Regularly appreciating what we already have in life gives us a feeling of abundance, leading to enhanced happiness and satisfaction. As the focus is on what we have rather than what we lack, it can also reduce stress levels. With such a focus, we are more likely to remain hopeful and optimistic, contributing to our happiness and well-being. Counting our blessings often leads us to express gratitude to people who have helped us, leading to better relationships.

During tough times, we build resilience by acknowledging positive aspects of life. With higher resilience, we can bounce back from trauma and stress more quickly, boosting our happiness. Appreciating what we have generates more positive emotions, contributing to well-being and satisfaction, while counting our blessings can also weaken the assumption that material possessions will make us happier. This leads to a more stable, authentic sense of happiness.

Scientific evidence

The broaden-and-build theory – a model of positive emotions developed by Professor Barbara Fredrickson – suggests that experiencing positive emotions leads to a broadening of cognitive abilities and a deepening of social support, resilience, skills and knowledge.[2] These enhanced resources then contribute to greater happiness, health and fulfilment. Following this theory, appreciating what we have can broaden our awareness of more positive aspects of our lives.

Cognitive-behavioural theory argues that focusing on blessings and the positive aspects of our lives helps us to reframe cognitive patterns towards more optimistic and grateful thinking, leading to reduced low mood and greater happiness. Recent research also suggests that counting one's blessings can reduce the negative effects of stress, with long-term benefits for mental health. Appreciation also fosters well-being and success indirectly, through forging and maintaining social bonds, promoting better sleep, encouraging helping and building trust.

Cultivating appreciation

There are many ways to cultivate greater appreciation in and of one's life, as summarized in Table 1.1. It is well worth investing time to build the habit of expressing gratitude to whatever is meaningful for you – whether it be other people, God, nature or something else – for all the blessings you enjoy in the different aspects of your life. Celebrate small accomplishments and learn to focus on moments of joy that can reinforce the habit of appreciation. Such activities can help to shift our focus away from what we lack and towards what we have and cherish.

---

2   Fredrickson, 2001

Writing about 'three good things' that happened during the day has been recommended as a practical way to cultivate appreciation.[3] This can be done daily, before bed, or weekly. It has been used in many studies as an intervention for enhancing happiness. Throughout the day or week, keep cues – such as photos, notes or mental images – to remind you when you come to write about your three good things. You could also set aside some time to think about or write down the positive aspects, experiences and people who have supported you in your life.

Performing acts of kindness can reinforce the positive feelings linked with blessings. The practice of giving thanks before eating meals is, for those who follow it, a way to acknowledge the blessing of having food on your plate. Likewise, visiting spiritual or religious places to offer prayers and give thanks – in whatever form your belief takes – can enhance the emotions associated with positive aspects of life. Sometimes there is no need to go anywhere – you can just close your eyes and acknowledge all the good things, positive aspects, uplifting experiences and generous people that you are lucky enough to have in your life.

Table 1.1: Key activities for cultivating appreciation

Activity	Description
Expressing gratitude	Cultivate the habit of expressing thanks for life's blessings.
'Three good things'	Write about three positive things that happened during the day, preferably before sleeping.
Weekly reflection	This activity can also be done weekly to cultivate appreciation.
Cues for reminders	Use photos, notes or mental imagery as cues to remind yourself of your blessings.
Positive reflection time	Set aside time to think about or write down positive experiences and supportive people.

---

3   Passmore & Oades, 2022

Celebrating small wins	Acknowledge and celebrate small wins and joyful moments.
Thanking before meals	Follow the practice of giving thanks for having food.
Spiritual visits	Visit spiritual or religious places to express gratitude.
Mental appreciation	Simply close your eyes and acknowledge the positive aspects of your life.

Appreciation doesn't always have to stem from grand events or achievements. Often, it is found in the simplicity of everyday life – good health, a loving family, a faithful pet. It can emerge from different areas of life, whether it's the support of loved ones, the joy of pursuing passions, or moments of spiritual connection such as a shared joke or a beautiful sunset. When we pause to appreciate life's blessings, we shift our focus to abundance and joy.

Personal vignette

I always appreciate and feel grateful for the people – be they family, friends or loved ones – who make my life richer and more beautiful. Sometimes more challenging too, but overall, they add meaning to my life. So many people have supported me in different ways. Sometimes, as a family, we discuss the positive things we have and the goodness of those who have supported us. Doing this has hugely impacted our overall happiness and satisfaction.

A brief activity for cultivating appreciation

Set aside a specific time to practice appreciation. Do it with family members if possible. Plan to invest just a few minutes in this activity. You can start by acknowledging things in your daily life. Think of the people who support you, the things that make your life convenient. Consider nature and other resources that support your existence and well-being. Think of all the happiness you already have. Acknowledge the breath that keeps you alive, and the body that enables you to experience and enjoy the world around you. Acknowledge your own capabilities. See the joy in everyday experiences. Realize that the whole universe is supporting you in so many ways. Appreciating what you have will always work its magic – lifting your mood and well-being.

Reflective questions

1. Explore some of the positive aspects you have in your life.
2. Think about how appreciation will affect your happiness.
3. Make a list of people who helped you to become who you are.
4. Think of blessings that you may not have acknowledged before.
5. Consider how your life would be different if some people and things were not present.
6. What did you learn from Birgitte's story?
7. What did you learn from Iain's story?

References and further reading

Adler, M. G., & Fagley, N. S. (2005) Appreciation: Individual differences in finding value and meaning as a unique predictor of subjective well-being. *Journal of Personality*, 73, 79-114.

Bhadra, S., & Dyer, A. R. (2022) Resilience and well-being among the survivors of natural disasters and conflicts. In: *Handbook of Health and Well-being: challenges, strategies and future trends* (pp. 637-667). Singapore: Springer Nature Singapore.

Beck, A. T. (1979) *Cognitive Therapy and the Emotional Disorders*. Penguin.

Cohn, M. A., Fredrickson, B. L., Brown, S. L., Mikels, J. A., & Conway, A. M. (2009) Happiness unpacked: positive emotions increase life satisfaction by building resilience. *Emotion*, 9(3), 361.

Dalai Lama, X. I. V., & Cutler, H. C. (1998) *The Art of Happiness: A handbook for living*. New York: Riverhead Books.

Emmons, R. A., & McCullough, M. E. (2003) Counting blessings versus burdens: an experimental investigation of gratitude and subjective well-being in daily life. *Journal of Personality and Social Psychology*, 84(2), 377.

Emmons, R. A., & Mishra, A. (2011) Why gratitude enhances well-being: What we know, what we need to know. In: K. M. Sheldon, T. B. Kashdan, & M. F. Steger (Eds.), *Designing Positive Psychology: Taking stock and moving forward* (pp. 248–262). Oxford: Oxford University Press.

Fagley, N. S., & Adler, M. G. (2012) Appreciation: A spiritual path to finding value and meaning in the workplace. *Journal of Management, Spirituality & Religion*, 9(2), 167-187.

Fredrickson, B. L. (2001) The role of positive emotions in positive psychology: The broaden-and-build theory of positive emotions. *American psychologist*, 56(3), 218.

Kardas, F., Cam, Z., Eskısu, M., & Gelıbolu, S. (2019) Gratitude, hope, optimism and life satisfaction as predictors of psychological well-being. *Eurasian Journal of Educational Research*, 19(82), 81-100.

Krejtz, I., Nezlek, J. B., Michnicka, A., Holas, P., & Rusanowska, M. (2016) Counting one's blessings can reduce the impact of daily stress. *Journal of Happiness Studies*, 17, 25-39.

Passmore, J., & Oades, L. G. (2022) Positive psychology techniques – Three Good Things. *Coaching Practiced*, 473-475.

Ryan, C. T. (2012) *A Mindful Nation: How a simple practice can help us reduce stress, improve performance, and recapture the American spirit*. Hay House, Inc.

Seligman, M. E. (2011) *Flourish: A visionary new understanding of happiness and well-being*. Simon and Schuster.

Sirgy, M. J. (2012) The psychology of quality of life: Hedonic well-being, life satisfaction, and eudaimonia (Vol. 50). Springer science & business media.

Swami, V., Voracek, M., Todd, J., Furnham, A., Horne, G., & Tran, U. S. (2024) Positive self-beliefs mediate the association between body appreciation and positive mental health. *Body Image*, 48, 101685.

Tsang, J. A., Carpenter, T. P., Roberts, J. A., Frisch, M. B., & Carlisle, R. D. (2014) Why are materialists less happy? The role of gratitude and need satisfaction in the relationship between materialism and life satisfaction. *Personality and Individual Differences*, 64, 62-66.

Waugh, C. E., & Koster, E. H. (2015) A resilience framework for promoting stable remission from depression. *Clinical Psychology Review*, 41, 49-60.

B

Chapter 2:

Bonding

'True happiness arises, in the first place, from the enjoyment of one's self, and in the next, from the friendship and conversation of a few select companions.'

Joseph Addison

According to Nobel laureate Daniel Kahneman, happiness is the experience of spending time with people you love and who love you.[4] Like food and air, we need social relationships to thrive. Feeling loved and giving out all the love we have is the root of happiness. A simple activity gives us so much pleasure when we do it with someone we

---

4   Kahneman, 2011

love and who loves us. It's not the activity, it's the person. Life can be beautiful, and the principal reason for that is the people we love. Even during tough times, just having someone to help us laugh things off and cope with it all together can be such a comfort.

Bonding is a process of having positive and sustainable relationships with warm and trustworthy people. Bonding is a basic need for all of us, and it plays an important role in happiness and health. Bonding is like oxygen, which is essential not only to surviving but also to thriving. By receiving continuous support from bonding, we can thrive in life. When we bond with others, we realize that we aren't alone with our problems. Bonding lightens life's burdens, making us feel happier than before. When we face difficult situations, bonding with people helps us to bounce back and survive. Just sharing our concerns with others helps us feel better. Conversely, a lack of bonding with people can be a significant factor behind emotional loneliness. We have a fundamental drive to create and maintain friendly social bonds. Having positive relationships with others is a key element of popular models of psychological well-being. On this basis, it might reasonably be argued that bonding is the single most significant factor in enhancing our happiness.

Bonding brings connection, trust and shared joy. Tim Anstiss's journey from solo competition to team sports reveals the deep happiness that can be found in togetherness:

As a young man I had some success in track and field, specifically the pole vault. I won several national titles and represented my country at senior level at seventeen. Athletics is an individual sport, and success typically depends on your level of skill, motivation and luck on the day.

At university, I began to play American football as a middle linebacker. On one play, I rushed past the offensive line and hit the running back in the backfield so hard he dropped the ball for a big loss. My teammates swarmed round and shouted "Yeah!", high-fiving and hugging me.

I was suddenly hit by an emotion I hadn't felt before in all my years of competing at track and field – a sense of bonding, of blending with others, of closeness and togetherness. And in that moment, I suddenly realized one of the reasons so many people play team sports.

Tim's story reminds us that true happiness often comes from shared experiences. Achievements feel richer when celebrated together, and bonds formed through teamwork create lasting fulfilment. In the end, it's not just about winning – it's about belonging.

Bonding and happiness

Social bonds are the most meaningful contributor to happiness. According to psychologist Martin Seligman, other people are the best antidote to the downs of life and the single most reliable 'up'.[5] Bonding helps us share our concerns with other people, leading to a reduction in stress and enhanced happiness. By investing in social connections, we find it easier to interpret adversity as a path to growth and opportunity. When we do have to experience stress, we bounce back from it faster, and we are better protected against its long-term negative effects. When we invest in our social support systems, we are simply better equipped to thrive in even the most difficult circumstances; while those who withdraw from people around them effectively cut off their lines of protection, at the very moment they need them most.

When we have strong bonds, we feel more able to seek help from others, helping us to achieve our goals. People with whom we have a strong bond listen and understand us. They don't judge us, and we feel safe and secure in sharing our concerns with them. They also try to give us much-needed hope in challenging situations. This renewed hope can help us to start striving for difficult goals and persisting during the more difficult phases of goal achievement.

Bonding with others makes us happy, as it reminds us that we are not alone. When we share a joke, open up about our personal struggles or celebrate small wins with people who care, it feels good. Being around people who truly see and support us makes life easier to handle and a lot more joyful. Bonds aren't just about talking, they're about knowing that someone is there for us, no matter what. These moments of closeness and belongingness, big or small, are what make life feel meaningful and full of love. When we share moments, laugh, or even face challenges together, we feel loved and valued. It's like having

---

5   Seligman, 2011

people who've got our back, which makes life feel easier and more joyful. For this reason, close relationships are considered the most important aspect of overall well-being in today's world.

Bonding boosts mood and allows us to understand other people's perspectives. Close relationships bring a sense of togetherness and help us fight loneliness. The more we feel connected to the people around us, the more we find positive interactions and a trusting environment which will ultimately light the way to well-being. Table 2.1 shows the various ways in which bonding enhances happiness.

Table 2.1: How bonding enhances happiness

Aspect of bonding	How it enhances happiness
Emotional support	Other people are the best antidote to life's ups and downs, and the most reliable source of uplifting.
Stress reduction	Sharing concerns reduces stress and enhances happiness.
Resilience building	Social connections help us interpret adversity as growth and enable quicker recovery from stress.
Thriving in difficult times	A strong support system equips us to thrive, while isolation removes vital support.
Goal achievement	Strong bonds encourage help-seeking, fostering motivation and persistence in goals.
Feeling understood and accepted	People with strong bonds listen without judgement, making us feel safe and secure.
Renewed hope	Supportive relationships offer encouragement during tough times, helping initiate and sustain goals.

Sense of belonging	Bonding reminds us that we are not alone, enhancing happiness.
Positive shared experiences	Laughing, sharing struggles and celebrating wins with others increases joy.
Emotional security	Knowing someone has our back makes life easier and more fulfilling.
Boosts mood and perspective	Close bonds improve mood and help us understand different perspectives.
Fights loneliness	Strong relationships foster togetherness, reducing loneliness and increasing happiness.
Trust and a positive environment	Feeling connected enhances trust and positive interactions, leading to happiness.

Scientific evidence

Research evidence suggests that if we have a best friend at work, we are much more productive and deliver far better results. Groundbreaking research by Roy Baumeister and Mark Leary found that: *"People form social attachments readily under most conditions and resist the dissolution of existing bonds. Belongingness appears to have multiple and strong effects on emotional patterns and on cognitive processes. Lack of attachments is linked to a variety of ill effects on health, adjustment, and well-being."*[6]

According to social support theory, strong social bonds act as a buffer against stress and loneliness and enhance resilience, leading to higher happiness and overall life satisfaction. When we experience stress, social bonds act as a cushion that softens the emotional blow. Different types of support such as emotional support, financial support, skill-building and so on help us to bounce back and cope better with challenging situations in future.

Self-determination theory suggests that humans have three needs: autonomy, competence and relatedness. Fulfilling these leads to well-

6   Baumeister & Leary, 1995

being. Of the three, the need for 'relatedness' refers to the need to feel connected and have close and caring relationships. Fulfilling this through social bonding and connections leads to optimal functioning and enhanced happiness. When we receive support from others, it helps us to become better in whatever we do and raises our confidence, leading to greater competence. Warm and trusting relationships also empower us to exercise autonomy and make our own choices. Thus, bonding helps us to satisfy all three needs of autonomy, competence and relatedness, enhancing our well-being.

A study using seventy years of evidence on adult development emphasized that our relationships with other people matter, and matter more than anything else in the world.[7] The social support we get from bonding with others prevents stress from knocking us down and getting in the way of us achieving our goals. Our social ties help us capitalize on our own strengths – to accomplish more in our work and in our lives. Each connection we make lowers our levels of cortisol, a hormone related to stress, which helps us recover faster from work-related stress and makes us better prepared to handle it in the future. Conversely, when we make a positive social connection, the pleasure-inducing hormone oxytocin is released into our bloodstream, immediately reducing anxiety and improving concentration and focus. Each social connection also bolsters our cardiovascular, neuroendocrine and immune systems, so that the more connections we make over time, the better we function. People with strong relationships are also less likely to perceive situations as stressful in the first place. Social interactions jolt us with positivity in the moment; then, each of these single connections strengthens a relationship over time, which raises our baseline happiness permanently.

All of us want to sustain desired changes in our lives, and in his book *The Science of Change* Professor Richard Boyatzis emphasizes that change is more likely to be sustained when we build and nurture positive relationships.[8] He argues that strong, supportive connections

---

7   Vaillant, 2009
8   Boyatzis, 2024

with others not only foster personal growth, but also provide the encouragement and accountability needed for lasting transformation. Thus, bonding can help us to create sustainable happiness.

Cultivating bonding

Bonding increases when we spend time together without distractions such as phones and social media. The best way to enhance bonding is to listen to people, understand their points of view, and enhance their efficacy and hope by encouraging them to express their thoughts, feelings and concerns freely and openly. Extending support to others enhances positive relationships. Sharing your time, attention and resources enhances bonding, as does taking part in group activities and attending community events together. Talking to people about their dreams and aspirations can also develop strong bonds. Conversations about dreams for the future lead to lifelong positive relationships. And, of course, being generous – whether with your time, money or other resources – also strengthens bonds of friendship.

In the world of work, bonding is essential for building effective teams and finding fulfilment in one's job. Having shared goals and activities creates great opportunities to enhance bonding between you and other people, although respecting others' needs and boundaries is crucial for maintaining these bonds. Leaders should ask their team members who they enjoy working with, who they share common goals with, and who they would like to partner with on future projects. People can also be encouraged to work together on shared community goals. Creating regular opportunities for people to get to know one another through their work is a great way to contribute to bonding.

Personal vignette

I have worked on projects and in organizations with a wide variety of people from all walks of life. In many cases strong bonds were developed that I still cherish and nurture today; but, on other occasions, this did not happen. So just spending time together is not enough to guarantee bonding. True bonding goes beyond mere interaction; it thrives on working with shared purpose, being authentic and keeping the well-being of others in mind.

A brief activity for cultivating bonding

Invite a family member or friend to spend time with you without any distractions such as phones, TV or social media. Spend the time sharing your personal experiences, talking about special events, or recalling previous happy times you've spent together. Plan to do this at least twice a month. Assess the impact of this activity on your mood, and on your relationship with the other person. Explore how the impact can be enhanced for similar activities in future.

Reflective questions

1. Who are the people with whom you enjoy authentic bonding? How frequently do you spend time with them?
2. How do you ensure you spend time with your loved ones with minimal distractions?
3. What type of shared activities lead to enhanced happiness for you?
4. Recall four to five occasions when you were having strong bonding experiences with people. What lessons can you apply to strengthen your bonding with new people in new contexts?
5. How can you contribute the most to enhance your bonds with the people you choose?
6. What did you learn from Tim's story?

References and further reading

Achor, S. (2010) *The Happiness Advantage: The seven principles that fuel success and performance at work*. New York, NY: Crown Business.

Baumeister, R. F., & Leary, M. R. (1995) The need to belong: Desire for interpersonal attachments as a fundamental human motivation. *Psychological Bulletin*, 117(3), 497–529. https://doi.org/10.1037/0033-2909.117.3.497

Boyatzis, R. E. (2024) *The Science of Change: Discovering how individuals, organizations, and communities can transform*. Oxford University Press.

Carlson, D. S., & Perrewé, P. L. (1999) The role of social support in the stressor-strain relationship: An examination of work-family conflict. *Journal of Management*, 25(4), 513-540.

Chayko, M. (2012) Connecting: How we form social bonds and communities in the Internet age. State University of New York Press.

Clifton, J., & Harter, J. (2021) *Wellbeing at Work: How to build resilience and mental health in your team*. New York, NY: Gallup Press.

Diener, E., & Biswas-Diener, R. (2011) *Happiness: Unlocking the mysteries of psychological wealth*. John Wiley & Sons.

Good, A., & Russo, F. A. (2022) Changes in mood, oxytocin, and cortisol following group and individual singing: A pilot study. *Psychology of Music*, 50(4), 1340-1347.

Hassanli, N., Walters, T., & Williamson, J. (2021) 'You feel you're not alone': how multicultural festivals foster social sustainability through multiple psychological sense of community. *Journal of Sustainable Tourism*, 29(11-12), 1792-1809.

Heaphy, E. D., & Dutton, J. E. (2008) Positive social interactions and the human body at work: Linking organizations and physiology. *Academy of Management Review*, 33(1), 137-162.

Kahneman, D. (2011) *Thinking, Fast and Slow*. New York, NY: Farrar, Straus and Giroux.

Rubin, G. (2009) *The Happiness Project: Or, why I spent a year trying to sing in the morning, clean my closets, fight right, read Aristotle, and generally have more fun*. HarperCollins.

Ryff, C. D. (1989) Happiness is everything, or is it? Explorations on the meaning of psychological well-being. *Journal of Personality and Social Psychology*, 57(6), 1069.

Seligman, M. E. P. (2011) *Flourish: A visionary new understanding of happiness and well-being*. New York, NY: Atria Books.

Vaillant, G. (2009, July 16) Yes, I stand by my words, "Happiness equals love—full stop." *Positive Psychology News*. Available at: https://positivepsychologynews.com/news/george-vaillant/200907163163 (accessed April 2025).

C

Chapter 3:
Collaborating

Sahakāriṇi kāryāṇi sahakāreṇa siddhayanti
Collaborative efforts lead to successful outcomes.

Ancient Indian wisdom

Human beings are social creatures, and our happiness is often intertwined with how we collaborate and connect with others. From ancient wisdom to modern science, there is ample evidence that coming together, sharing efforts and working towards common goals not only helps us achieve desired outcomes, but also enhances happiness.

Whether it is families working together, friends playing games or colleagues brainstorming ideas, collaboration has the potential to transform ordinary tasks into extraordinary experiences.

Collaboration is like rain forming a river – small efforts combine to create a powerful flow that nourishes everyone. I have realized that taking a moment to have a cup of coffee with a colleague during a hectic day is always a refreshing experience. On a larger scale, I am always filled with energy and enthusiasm whenever I am able to take part in Indian festival celebrations. When I am engaged in shared activities, it almost always enhances my happiness.

In their best-selling book *Ikigai*, Héctor García and Francesc Miralles note that playing and celebrating as a community is essential to well-being and satisfaction.[9] Collaboration enhances everyone's happiness. Collaboration can be defined as working together to achieve common objectives. These might be especially big or difficult goals, leisure activities, or even simple everyday activities like watching TV together. It is not only about formal work-related collaborations – there can be informal social collaborations as well.

Collaborating requires coordination, cooperation, communication, trust and respect among the participating group members. When we work together, we pool our skills and resources to achieve common objectives. Working together enhances overall creative output, leading to better decisions and eventual outcomes. This in turn enhances the happiness of all involved.

> **Collaboration comes in many forms, ranging from the professional to the personal. And it is often about helping others find the right way forward for them, as this story from Rajiv Naithani shows:**
>
> *To me, happiness isn't loud. It's not always celebratory. It's often quiet, internal, and rooted in clarity and peace, especially when it follows collaboration grounded in trust and mutual respect.*

---

9   García & Miralles, 2017

One such experience unfolded not in a boardroom, but at home. My daughter was starting her secondary education, navigating that beautiful and confusing teenage phase. As parents working in the technology industry, my wife and I were naturally inclined toward encouraging a STEM/Science stream, because we believed it would open foundational doors for her. But my daughter wasn't keen. She had observed us over the years – the long workdays, the demanding nature of technology roles – and to her, it seemed unexciting and exhausting.

A tension had started to build between her and my wife. It was less about subjects, and more about what kind of life she envisioned for herself. I realized it had to step in. And, instead of telling her what to do, I chose to collaborate. We sat down and had a heartfelt conversation. I asked her to imagine herself in the future: "What does success look like to you? What kind of life do you want to create?" Her answer was clear and mature beyond her years: "I see myself as a successful woman leader, someone who creates, maybe even an entrepreneur." I reflected that back: "So who usually creates things? What kind of learning journey do they take?"

She went off, thought about it, did her own research. A few days later, she came back and said, "Most of the people I looked at have a tech foundation. They understand how things work, then build on it and maybe do an MBA later." She had reached the conclusion we hoped for, but this time, it was hers. The happiness I felt wasn't because she chose STEM/Science. It was because she made an informed, self-owned decision, and as a parent, I found peace in her clarity.

That moment reinforced a deeper truth that I've also experienced at work. During situations like M&A integrations, when emotions and uncertainty run high, it's easy to slip into a control mindset. But the real breakthrough happens when we invite people to co-create, not comply. "Your company is not becoming our company. We're becoming something new – together."

> *Whether it's your child, a junior colleague, or a newly acquired team, the most powerful thing you can do is trust their mind, hold space for their voice, and let collaboration lead the way. Because in the end, true happiness isn't in making the right decision for someone, it's in watching them make the right decision for themselves.*

Rajiv's touching account of how a potential source of tension was transformed into a fertile discussion that made a family stronger is a reminder of how collaboration can bring people together, and of its power to create happiness far beyond traditional workplace settings.

Collaboration and happiness

When we participate in enjoyable shared activities with other people, these activities often elicit positive emotions such as joy, enthusiasm and excitement, leading to enhanced well-being. Collaboration can also help us to achieve daunting or difficult goals, leading to a sense of accomplishment and fulfilment. Working together gives us feelings of companionship and connectedness, and enjoying a shared activity can reduce stress and other mental health symptoms such as anxiety and depression. All of this promotes emotional health and happiness. Collaboration with others to work towards shared goals also has the potential to enhance our interpersonal relationships, contributing to life satisfaction, and to enhance components of psychological capital such as self-efficacy, hope, resilience and optimism.

Scientific evidence

A study conducted by Harry Reis and colleagues, titled 'Fun is more fun when others are involved', found that sharing activities creates more intense emotions than working alone.[10] Sharing pleasant experiences, in real time or by talking about them, typically has the effect of amplifying and prolonging our pleasures. Whether we exercise, commute or do housework, everything is more fun in company. Researchers have also found that eating together improves the well-being of family members.[11]

---

10   Reis *et al.*, 2017
11   Eisenberg *et al.*, 2004

A recent international study including participants from the US, Italy, and Germany found that a higher frequency of shared family meals correlated with fewer depressive symptoms, more connectedness and higher levels of happiness in adults.[12]

Collaboration can foster a sense of belonging, which is a powerful predictor of whether a person finds their life meaningful. Collaborating towards shared group goals also enhances an individual's sense of social well-being in key dimensions such as social integration and social contribution; in addition, working together increases our chances of fulfilling the three needs of self-determination theory – autonomy, competence and relatedness – discussed in the last chapter. Overall, there is a strong positive association between collaboration and happiness.

Cultivating collaboration

Collaboration can be enhanced by encouraging participation and identifying opportunities for people to reach for shared objectives. Building trust and psychological safety among everyone involved is a crucial factor for enhanced and sustained collaboration.

To cultivate a spirit of healthy collaboration, it's important to:

- Set clear goals and make sure there are opportunities for feedback.
- Celebrate progress and wins to help maintain the morale of the group.
- Ensure adequate resources and support for team members.
- Clearly define roles and responsibilities to avoid confusion and empower the group.
- Encourage ongoing reflection and adaptation to foster a culture of continuous learning and improvement.
- Make use of collaboration tools and techniques to enhance communication, build trust and resolve any conflicts that arise.

Sometimes there can be challenges in collaborating with others – such as miscommunication, conflict or lack of common objectives. These can be handled by paying careful attention to their causes and

---

12   Berge *et al.*, 2024

inviting members to talk to each other and understand the issues. Team members can also seek mentoring and coaching support to help them handle these challenges. Table 3.1 depicts the 'building blocks' of effective collaboration.

Table 3.1: Building blocks of effective collaboration

Key element	Description
Identifying shared objectives	Aligning goals to ensure everyone works towards a common purpose.
Encouraging participation	Actively involving all members to contribute ideas and efforts.
Building trust and psychological safety	Creating an environment where members feel safe to express their thoughts.
Setting clear goals and feedback	Defining expectations and providing regular feedback for improvement.
Celebrating progress	Recognizing achievements to boost morale and motivation.
Defining roles and responsibilities	Clarifying duties to avoid confusion and enhance efficiency.
Ongoing reflection and adaptation	Learning from experiences and making continuous adjustments.
Using collaboration tools and techniques	Leveraging technology and strategies for effective teamwork.

Personal vignette

When I was young, on winter evenings the cold used to seep through the cracks in the windows of our house. During those times, my family peeled peas to keep warm. My father would come home with a big bag of peas, and we would all peel them and talk for hours on end. No one ever felt tired – we enjoyed it. Working together, and connecting rather than just completing, transformed an ordinary experience into something meaningful and joyful.

A brief activity for cultivating collaboration

Invite a small group of people to engage in a shared enjoyable activity. Suggest a few options and set out the time involved. Choose the type of activity according to the group you are inviting. Once the group has completed the shared activity, ask each member to assess the impact of the activity on their happiness. Then invite everyone to give their feedback – to share how the activity made them feel, and how it affected their sense of connection and happiness. Finally, decide on a plan for engaging in similar shared activities going forward.

Reflective questions

1. How often have you engaged in in enjoyable shared activities with other people in the last fourteen days?

2. Can you recall any shared activities that you used to enjoy but have allowed to lapse?

3. Think of two or three shared activities through which you can contribute to the world in a positive way.

4. How could you initiate more collaborative activities in your personal life or at work?

5. What ordinary experiences might become extraordinary if you worked with others?

References and further reading

Berge, J. M., Doherty, W. J., Klemenhagen, K. C., Hersch, D., Mendenhall, T. J., & Danner, C. (2024) A descriptive examination of international family/shared meals: Prevalence, meal types, media at meals, and emotional well-being. *Families, Systems, & Health.*

Connor, M., & Pokora, J. (2017) *Coaching and Mentoring at Work: Developing effective practice: Developing effective practice.* McGraw-Hill Education (UK).

Eisenberg, M. E., Olson, R. E., Neumark-Sztainer, D., Story, M., & Bearinger, L. H. (2004) Correlations between family meals and psychosocial well-being among adolescents. *Archives of Pediatrics & Adolescent Medicine,* 158(8), 792-796.

Gable, S. L., Reis, H. T., Impett, E. A., & Asher, E. R. (2018) *What Do You Do When Things Go Right? The intrapersonal and interpersonal benefits of sharing positive events.* In: L. M. Cooper & D. M. H. Knapp (Eds.), *Relationships, Well-being, and Behavior* (pp. 144–182). Routledge.

García, H., & Miralles, F. (2017) *Ikigai: The Japanese secret to a long and happy life.* Penguin.

Huang, X., & Wang, C. (2021) Factors affecting teachers' informal workplace learning: The effects of school climate and psychological capital. *Teaching and Teacher Education,* 103, 103363.

Hussein, B. (2021) Addressing collaboration challenges in project-based learning: The student's perspective. *Education Sciences,* 11(8), 434.

Kahn, P., Goodhew, P., Murphy, M., & Walsh, L. (2013) The Scholarship of Teaching and Learning as collaborative working: A case study in shared practice and collective purpose. *Higher Education Research & Development,* 32(6), 901-914.

Keyes, C. L. M. (1998) *Social well-being. Social Psychology Quarterly,* 121-140.

Kun, A., & Gadanecz, P. (2022) Workplace happiness, well-being and their relationship with psychological capital: A study of Hungarian Teachers. *Current Psychology,* 41(1), 185-199.

Lambert, N. M., Stillman, T. F., Hicks, J. A., Kamble, S., Baumeister, R. F., & Fincham, F. D. (2013). To belong is to matter: Sense of belonging enhances meaning in life. *Personality and Social Psychology Bulletin,* 39(11), 1418-1427.

Luthans, F., & Youssef, C. M. (2004) Human, social, and now positive psychological capital management: Investing in people for competitive advantage. University of Nebraska.

Mattessich, P. W., & Johnson, K. M. (2018) *Collaboration: What makes it work.* Fieldstone Alliance.

Prilleltensky, I., & Prilleltensky, O. (2021) *How People Matter: Why it affects health, happiness, love, work, and society.* Cambridge University Press.

Reis, H. T., O'Keefe, S. D., & Lane, R. D. (2017) Fun is more fun when others are involved. *The Journal of Positive Psychology,* 12(6), 547–557.

Rubin, G. (2009) *The Happiness Project: Or, why I spent a year trying to sing in the morning, clean my closets, fight right, read Aristotle, and generally have more fun.* HarperCollins.

Ryan, R. M., & Deci, E. L. (2000) Self-determination theory and the facilitation of intrinsic motivation, social development, and well-being. *American Psychologist,* 55(1), 68-78.

Toni, M., Mehta, A. K., Chandel, P. S., Kamalakkannan, M. K., & Selvakumar, P. (2025) Mentoring and Coaching in Staff Development. In: *Innovative Approaches to Staff Development in Transnational Higher Education* (pp. 1-26). IGI Global Scientific Publishing.

D

Chapter 4:
Digital detox

"Almost everything will work again if you unplug it for a few minutes... including you."

Anne Lamott

These days, the first thing that most of us touch in the morning is not a loved one's hand – it's a phone. We scroll endlessly without purpose. Notifications pull us away from conversations. In this hyper-connected world, our minds are rarely at rest. Minds are like still water – clear and reflective. But constant digital noise stirs the surface, making it murky. A digital detox allows the mind to settle, restoring its natural clarity. It allows us to disconnect in order to reconnect.

If you give up your phone for a brief period and instead look for other technology-free ways to spend your time, you can reconnect with the real world. Activities like spending time outside in nature, going for a walk or reading a book will give you a sense of purpose that is lost when you are endlessly engaged in the digital world. When you are not glued to a screen, you can experience moments of true connection with others, which will enhance your happiness.

Technology is reducing our attention span, because there is so much fast-paced content out there. It is getting harder to concentrate on simple tasks. So, the need for a digital detox now is greater than ever. The purpose of it is press pause: to decrease the irresistible use of digital devices and instead achieve a balance between online and offline activities. A digital detox lets us focus on self-reflection and real-life interactions with family, friends and colleagues.

The duration of a digital detox depends on your digital detoxification goals and your preferences, and it may vary from a few hours to several days. A break from digital devices can rejuvenate your emotional well-being, clearing space in your mental garden – pulling out weeds of distraction so that attention, connection and happiness can bloom.

Digital detox and happiness

Constant connectivity to digital devices creates stress, and it can lead us to feel overwhelmed and anxious. Taking a break from screen time can reduce stress and give relief, resulting in relaxation and rejuvenation. Disconnected from digital devices, we can be fully immersed in our experiences, giving us the space to interact with other people and to appreciate the present moment. The lack of distractions can also improve our productivity and mental health. During a digital detox, we are able to get in touch with our concerns and needs and prioritize satisfying those needs, leading to enhanced happiness and fulfilment.

In this account, coaching psychologist Andrea Giraldez-Hayes explores how she found a balance between technology's benefits and the need to unplug and reconnect with life:

Although I was born in the sixties, when technology was scarce, I've been passionate about it for as long as I can remember. I still recall, as a child, reading a science fiction article about how, in the future, people would be able to see each other on a telephone call. The images depicted large pods resembling phone booths, complete with seats and a big screen inside. I was fascinated, hoping that progress would occur before I grew too old.

What I never anticipated was that developments would happen much faster than predicted. In fact, in 1990, I acquired my first (quite large) cell phone. By 1995, I had my first modem, began exchanging texts with colleagues, and even managed to create my first website by copying and adapting the code I found in a magazine. When I commenced my PhD in 1996, I decided to investigate how the internet would transform our connections and learning experiences. Around that time, Pierre Lévy introduced the concept of collective intelligence, and I was captivated. Since then, I have eagerly followed every twist and turn of technological progress. The internet has opened doors we never thought possible.

However, there is a flip side. Being constantly connected comes at a cost. Continuous emails, social media pings, endless notifications and publications chip away at our ability to focus. We jump from one piece of information to the next, rarely giving our minds a chance to breathe. It's exhausting, even if we don't always realize it. And that's where the notion of a digital detox comes in – stepping back from screens, social media, and emails for a few days to reconnect with the physical and emotional world. The aim? To relieve stress and regain clarity. While science hasn't definitively proven that a digital detox is effective, some evidence suggests it can offer benefits such as reduced anxiety, improved sleep, and enhanced mental well-being. Many people, me included, find these advantages invaluable.

> *Let's face it though: pulling off a digital detox is far harder than it once was. A few years ago, we could unplug. Now, we pay with our phones, work on our laptops and maintain relationships through apps. The pandemic only deepened that bond with technology. Yet, every time I manage to unplug, even briefly, I feel a shift. A walk feels more vibrant without a podcast in my ear, and a conversation feels richer without my phone buzzing. Turning off notifications before reading or writing, designating tech-free time, making my bedroom a no-tech zone, embracing offline activities, and, when possible, taking days off and travelling without technology are just a few options I've already experienced, and will continue to try.*
>
> *After all, technology is powerful – but so is disconnecting.*

Taking breaks from technology enhances focus, reduces stress and deepens real-world connections. A digital detox isn't about avoiding technology; it's about creating space for clarity and well-being. By unplugging, we reclaim balance and invite greater happiness.

Scientific evidence

There is a good deal of research evidence showing that a technology-free life can aid our mental stress levels. Research has shown that even a brief digital detox can reduce stress and improve sleep and social interactions.[13] However, some research participants also faced challenges when digital detoxing – they were so addicted to social media and the instant gratification that comes with connecting with people online, that when they were cut off from the digital world, they began to feel isolated, alienated from others and bored. This was overcome, however, by engaging in more socially productive activities like volunteering.

In another study, titled 'Impacts of digital social media detox for mental health', the excessive use of social media was linked to anxiety, stress, depressive episodes and sleep disturbances.[14] A digital detox can reduce these problems; however, it is not a panacea. It will not 'cure' depression or significantly mitigate stress levels, and other practices

---

13   Coyne & Woodruff, 2023
14   Ramadhan *et al.*, 2024

like mindfulness should also be considered. The study also showed that while a digital detox has benefits for areas like depression, its effectiveness depends on the individual's mindset and wider behaviours.

According to psychologist Mihaly Csikszentmihalyi's Flow Theory, flow is a state of total immersion in an activity.[15] This total immersion in an enjoyable activity enhances happiness. A digital detox can lead us to engage ourselves in interesting and challenging offline activities, generating opportunities for flow. For example, during no-screen time, we might engage in drawing, sketching or playing an instrument – and these activities may induce a flow state. A digital detox also allows us to exercise autonomy around the use of our time and preferences for activities, leading to the fulfilment of the autonomy need of self-determining theory.

Mindfulness theory suggests that non-judgemental acceptance of the present moment may reduce stress and increase happiness. We will be more mindful if we disconnect from screens and pay full attention to the present moment, leading to higher well-being and satisfaction. For example, when we are engaged in reading a book without any distractions from screens, we can give our full attention to the pages in front of us. We may have similar mindful experiences while doing exercise or having a heart-to-heart conversation with a loved one.

Cultivating digital detox

Having clear intentions for a digital detox will inspire you to begin one. Create a digital-free zone in your home and keep all digital devices out of that space. Setting rules and boundaries around digital use may create more free time for family, friends, health and rejuvenation. This time can be used for hobbies, reading, exercise, spending time in nature, playing with kids and so on. How you choose to use it will give better results from your digital detox. You may set technology-free goals for your screen-free periods. Reducing the number of notifications on your digital devices may minimize distractions and help you focus on offline activities.

---

15   Csikszentmihalyi, 1990

Surround yourself with people who indulge in digital detoxes and encourage others to do the same. Their encouragement may motivate you to remain committed. Encouragement from others may also help you handle the anxiety some people experience when turning off their digital devices. You may wish to engage in 'digital-free evenings' by setting a specific time in the evening at which to switch off all devices and focus on self-care or family time.

Not using screens may initially cause you to feel bored or alienated, again challenging your commitment. To manage this issue, plan ahead for what to do during your digital detox – for instance, interacting with others or undertaking volunteer work. Seek suggestions from family and friends, and make lists of activities that you can look forward to enjoying when you turn off all your digital devices. One useful strategy is to have a jar for playful fun activities, written on small pieces of paper. Whenever you feel like checking your phone during your digital detox, you can choose a piece of paper and do that activity instead.

If you find the thought of time without your devices and connections worrying, you can reduce your screen time gradually. Start by turning off all your digital devices for just a few minutes per day. Then slowly increase until you eventually reach your desired level.

The flowchart below illustrates the path to digital balance – a step-by-step process to regain control over your screen time and establish digital well-being:

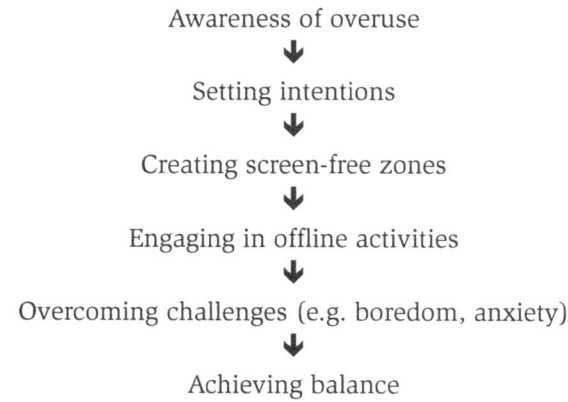

Awareness of overuse
⬇
Setting intentions
⬇
Creating screen-free zones
⬇
Engaging in offline activities
⬇
Overcoming challenges (e.g. boredom, anxiety)
⬇
Achieving balance

Personal vignette

When I leave my phone behind during my evening walk, I feel a refreshing sense of freedom. I can see the trees and flowers, and I can become fully absorbed in small interactions with the people I meet. I could never realize that peace when I was carrying a phone with all its distractions of constant notifications. When I compare my state of mind when taking a walk with a phone and without one, I notice that I am far more peaceful and relaxed without it.

A brief activity for cultivating digital detox

Go to a nearby park or a green space, leaving your digital devices at home or turning them all off. Now simply walk around, focusing on your surroundings. Pay attention to sounds, trees, leaves, flowers, water or birds. Sit mindfully for some time and focus on your breath. Scan your body and observe your bodily sensations.

Another activity to try is a 'no-screen evening' with family or friends. By using this time for activities that you all enjoy, such as playing games or having a picnic, you can generate shared moments, strengthen emotional bonds with your loved ones and create lasting memories.

Reflective questions

1. What would the benefits of a digital detox be for you?
2. How have you felt when you have disconnected yourself from digital devices in the past?
3. What will you do in the time when your digital devices are turned off?
4. How might your relationship with other people change due to a digital detox?
5. What small rituals can you create to embrace offline moments?
6. How does unplugging affect the quality of your conversations?
7. What do you discover about yourself in the absence of constant distractions?
8. What did you learn from Andrea's story?

References and further reading

Anandpara, G., Kharadi, A., Vidja, P., Chauhan, Y., Mahajan, S., & Patel, J. (2024) A comprehensive review on digital detox: A newer health and wellness trend in the current era. *Cureus*, 16(4).

Bajaj, B., & Pande, N. (2016) Mediating role of resilience in the impact of mindfulness on life satisfaction and affect as indices of subjective well-being. *Personality and Individual Differences*, 93, 63-67.

Bajaj, B., Khoury, B., & Sengupta, S. (2022) Resilience and stress as mediators in the relationship of mindfulness and happiness. *Frontiers in Psychology*, 13, 771263.

Bawden, D., & Robinson, L. (2009) The dark side of information: overload, anxiety and other paradoxes and pathologies. *Journal of Information Science*, 35(2), 180-191.

Coyne, P., & Woodruff, S. J. (2023). Taking a break: the effects of partaking in a two-week social media digital detox on problematic smartphone and social media use, and other health-related outcomes among young adults. *Behavioral Sciences*, 13(12), 1004.

Czikszentmihalyi, M. (1990) *Flow: The psychology of optimal experience* (pp. 75-77). New York: Harper & Row.

de la Fuente, V. (2022) *Digital Detox: Master your digital life: avoid distractions and anxiety, increase your productivity without stress and achieve mental calmness.* Víctor de la Fuente.

Miksch, L., & Schulz, C. (2018) Disconnect to Reconnect: The phenomenon of digital detox as a reaction to technology overload.

Nguyen, M. H., Büchi, M., & Geber, S. (2024) Everyday disconnection experiences: Exploring people's understanding of digital well-being and management of digital media use. *New Media & Society*, 26(6), 3657-3678.

Ramadhan, R. N., Rampengan, D. D., Yumnanisha, D. A., Setiono, S. B., Tjandra, K. C., Ariyanto, M. V., ... & Empitu, M. A. (2024) Impacts of digital social media detox for mental health: A systematic review and meta-analysis. *Narra J*, 4(2), e786.

Ryan, R. M., & Deci, E. L. (2000) Self-determination theory and the facilitation of intrinsic motivation, social development, and well-being. *American Psychologist*, 55(1), 68-78.

Sharma, A. K., & Sharma, R. (2024) Detox for success: how digital detoxification can enhance productivity and well-being. In: *Business Drivers in Promoting Digital Detoxification* (pp. 71-90). IGI Global.

Wasie, T. (2024) *Disconnect to Reconnect: Finding Balance to Reclaim Well-being.* Teshome Wasie.

Chapter 5:
Emotions

In his book *Emotional Intelligence: Why it can matter more than IQ*, Daniel Goleman emphasizes the power of understanding and managing emotions in all dimensions of work and life.[16] He argues that the ability to recognize, understand and manage our own emotions, as well as the ability to recognize, understand and influence the emotions of others, is crucial for effective leadership, relationships and overall well-being.

---

16   Goleman, 1995

There are three broad areas related to emotions that may affect our mental health and well-being: **understanding emotions, expressing emotions** and **managing emotions**. We need to work on all three to maintain our well-being, and all three go hand in hand with each other.

Understanding emotions includes understanding our own emotions as well as the emotions of others. When we are adept at understanding our own emotions, we can identify them in different situations, and we can understand the reasons for them at specific moments. We can also differentiate between similar emotions. When we understand our own emotions, we are able to recognize patterns in our emotional responses, and we become more aware of how our emotions can affect our actions and decisions. Similarly, when we understand others' emotions, we can often guess how someone is feeling based on their facial expressions, gestures, body language and paralinguistic communication. We can also sense emotional changes in the people around us. This helps us to understand how our words and actions impact others emotionally. Understanding others' emotions makes us more able to empathize with them, even when we haven't experienced their situations personally.

Expressing emotions refers to conveying one's feelings. Both positive and negative emotions are expressed through various channels such as verbal communication, facial expression and body language. The expression of emotion is a fundamental aspect of human communication. When we are adept at expressing emotions, we can openly and accurately express them in conversations, and we can express them in a way that is appropriate for the situation we are in. We can use also express our emotions through creative outlets such as writing, art or music.

Managing emotions is about regulating and managing emotions in social situations. When we are adept at this, we can stay calm and composed even when we experience strong emotions such as anger or frustration. We can manage emotions when dealing with difficult people or conflict, and we can manage stress in healthy ways rather than letting it overwhelm us. Skill at managing emotions also helps us to support others to manage their own emotions. With skilful emotional management, we can create a positive atmosphere in group settings. We can also help others to manage their own emotions by offering them support, reminding them of previous achievements, helping with work if they are overburdened, asking questions that inspire them to move forward, or simply listening to their concerns. Giving too much advice may not always be best, but we can give time and space to let others discover their own solutions. And, if it seems appropriate to us, we can encourage them to seek professional help.

Emotions and happiness

Understanding our emotions helps us to make better choices that align with our well-being. It helps us to understand our needs, our concerns and our values. Being aware of our positive emotions helps us to savour them and thereby enhance our well-being. Understanding others' emotions helps us support them when they need our support, contributing to better relationships and fulfilment. When we understand others' emotions, we are better able to help them manage their emotions. For example, if your friend is feeling down due to a recent failure, you might encourage them by showing confidence in their abilities. Understanding and joining others in their positive emotions strengthens our relationships with them.

Expressing emotions through words, art or actions releases emotional tensions and creates space for positivity. Talking, crying, journaling or even physical activity allows us to release the build-up of emotional energy. This can provide immediate relief and lighten the burden of unexpressed feelings, leading to reduced stress and a relaxed state of mind. Sharing emotions is also a powerful tool for bonding and strengthening social ties. When we share a negative emotional experience, we can receive help, support, comfort, consolation and validation, as well as advice and solutions contributing to enhanced happiness and satisfaction.

In their book *Expressing Emotions*, Eileen Kennedy-Moore and Jeanne C. Watson argue that emotional expression enables individuals to label and understand their emotions, and to extract information from them.[17] Labelling, understanding and extracting information fosters emotional insight, directs coping efforts and boosts well-being. Expressing positive emotions amplifies that positivity. When we express our emotions,

---

17   Kennedy-Moore & Watson, 2001

people often understand us better and may respond in constructive ways. Authentic expression of emotion allows us to live more genuinely, reducing internal conflicts and increasing a sense of fulfilment and joy.

Expressing emotions appropriately may help avoid conflict and enhance interpersonal relationships, leading to increased happiness and fulfilment. When emotions are expressed appropriately, we can better share our expectations – and sharing expectations and boundaries can help us to handle interpersonal problems and conflicts. For example, when one person in a couple shares their expectations without waiting for the other person to guess them, misunderstandings are avoided. Emotional sharing creates an environment in which people feel valued, understood and connected, which leads to happier, healthier lives.

Acknowledging emotions can greatly enhance our relationships and well-being. Here, Aitana Leret demonstrates the process of emotional acceptance and the peace it brings:

For a long time, I lived in quiet dissonance – outwardly composed but inwardly restless. I had learned to suppress my emotions, fearing they might disrupt the fragile balance of appearances. This inner divide left me fragmented, unable to fully rest in the simplicity of being.

One day, a friend said, "You're always listening to others, guiding them. But how are you, really?" Their words struck a chord. I felt the familiar pull to say, "I'm fine", but something deeper stirred – a longing to be honest. Instead of retreating into pretence, I confessed, "I feel overwhelmed and uncertain", and tears came.

In that moment, I let go of the need to protect or perfect myself. By simply acknowledging what I felt, I opened the door to a deeper connection – both with my friend and with myself. I realized that authenticity isn't about fixing or performing; it's about allowing what is real to be seen, without fear. Emotions, I've come to understand, are like waves – rising, cresting and passing away. When I stopped clinging to or resisting them, I discovered a profound peace.

Happiness, I realized, doesn't come from controlling emotions, but from knowing I am not defined by them. Beneath the waves, the ocean remains – vast, still, and whole.

Aitana's courage in allowing herself to be vulnerable, and in accepting and expressing her emotions, enabled her to foster a deeper connection with others and herself.

Unmanaged emotions can drain energy and happiness. By managing emotions, we prevent negative emotions from dominating our well-being and help ourselves bounce back from setbacks quickly. We reframe situations and act calmly with a balanced mindset. Handling emotions well – both our own and others – enhances social harmony. It reduces conflicts and fosters trust. And, as emotions are contagious, well-managed emotions create an uplifting atmosphere in personal and social settings, contributing to collective happiness.

Managing emotions includes shifting from negative to positive states when needed. By practicing gratitude, optimism and emotional reframing, we enhance our daily happiness. Beyond just regulating emotions, managing emotions includes generating positive emotions such as enthusiasm, inspiration and compassion, which enrich our lives and those of others.

This story from Jonathan Passmore beautifully illustrates how emotional management and reframing can turn a moment of frustration into an opportunity for peace and joy:

When our children were very small, I would take them at weekends to the supermarket to do the shopping. In the UK (and probably in many other parts of the world), supermarkets have parking bays marked out for parents and young children. On this occasion, I drove in, and the supermarket was busy. Maybe we were later than normal, but either way all the bays for parents and babies were taken apart from one.

I had the space in my sights, and I was indicating to pull in when a large 4x4 SUV coming from the other direction suddenly cut in front of us and stole the space. A tall, well-built man got out of the car and strode off towards the supermarket doors. There was no baby, toddler or child to be seen.

> *At that moment, I felt a flood of emotion: anger. I wanted to run over to the car, bang on the screen and tell him that as he did not have a baby the space was not for him. He should move and let parents with children park there. But being 5' 4" – compared with this man's 6' 6" – I wondered what the response would be. Probably a punch in the face or an expletive. Either way, this emotional hijack was not leading to happiness. I needed to reframe. Rather than jumping out of the car, I drove to the far side of the car park, parked, got my daughter out and into her buggy and we enjoyed the walk through the spring sunshine to the store.*
>
> *Events happen in life, and carrying this anger or emotion only damages us. We can seek retribution, or we can reframe our thinking – maybe the man was in a rush to get medication urgently needed by his partner – and then refocus on what gives us joy that we might not have seen or experienced had these events not happened.*

Jonathan's story exemplifies the power of managing emotions, and how doing so effectively gives us the ability to reframe frustrating situations and shift our focus towards what really matters. When we learn to regulate frustration, let go of unnecessary negativity and focus on joy, we create a happier and more fulfilling life for ourselves and those around us.

Scientific evidence

Emotional contagion theory suggests that we unconsciously mimic the emotions of others through non-verbal cues. By expressing our own emotions, we also impact the emotional experiences of other people. Therefore, expressing positive emotions spreads happiness to others in a ripple effect, leading to a more harmonious environment and enhanced well-being for everyone. For example, when an individual expresses enthusiasm, other people around them tend to mirror their expressions and feel enthusiastic themselves.

Broaden-and-build theory suggests that expressing positive emotions can broaden cognitive abilities and build resources such as social support, skills and resilience, which contributes to enhanced health and fulfilment.[18] Experiencing and expressing positive emotions can also help us to be more creative, find more solutions to handle problems and foster an open-minded attitude. Due to these expanded cognitive abilities, we adapt and respond better to life's challenges, leading to reduced stress and enhanced well-being. The regular expression of emotions not only boosts our current mood but also helps in building long-term satisfaction.

Changing emotional expression according to the situation at hand contributes to success and happiness. In a study of almost five hundred pitches for funding using computer-aided facial expression analysis, results showed an inverted U-shaped relationship between the frequency of facial expressions of happiness, anger and fear and funding.[19] There was a negative relationship between expressions of sadness and funding. The same research also suggested that moderate rather than low or very high levels of emotional expression can bring better results. Emotional expression research holds that the way in which an expression is received by others is shaped by display rules – social norms governing appropriate expression. Expressing emotions in healthy and constructive ways is the key to expressing emotions.

Cultivating emotions

The first step to enhancing emotional awareness is to reflect on different situations and how we respond to them. Seeking feedback from others on our emotional patterns may also assist our understanding. We can pay attention to our emotional responses by being mindful, or by maintaining a journal for writing our emotions down. Developing a wide emotion vocabulary may also help to identify and label our emotions. Observing others with an open mind can help us to understand their emotions – but rather than making any assumptions, it is useful to check with them how they feel at a particular point in time.

To enhance emotional expression, we can practice expressing emotions in an authentic manner and communicating them effectively. We can surround ourselves with supportive people, and we can work on

18   Fredrickson, 2001
19   Warnick *et al.*, 2021

developing trusting relationships so that we express our emotions without fear of rejection or judgement. Learning to express emotions through creative tools such as painting, poetry and other forms of art can also enhance emotional expression.

To enhance our emotional management, we can learn strategies to remain calm and composed during stressful situations. Engaging in mindfulness exercises, journaling or emotional check-ins can help us to recognize and regulate our emotions, and breathing and relaxation techniques may help us to regain emotional balance. Reinterpreting negative events in a more positive or neutral way can aid us in better managing our responses. Cultivate constructive outlets such as exercise, hobbies or talking with a trusted friend to channel your emotions productively.

Reframing negative emotions is a powerful mental shift that can transform challenges into opportunities, allowing us to navigate life with resilience and wisdom. The reframing cycle shown below illustrates how shifting perspectives can transform emotions – for example by turning frustration into growth, fear into courage, and setbacks into learning experiences.

Triggering event
Something happens that causes a negative emotion.

Initial negative emotion
For example: frustration, fear, anger.

Pause and awareness
Recognizing the emotion and its impact.

Reframing thought process
Changing perspective, finding meaning.

New positive perspective
For example: learning opportunity.

Emotional shift
Positive emotion like motivation, growth mindset.

Constructive action

Taking steps based on the new perspective

Cycle repeats

Strengthening the habit of reframing.

Now take a pause and think. Try to recall a recent frustrating situation and see if you can apply the reframing cycle to transform it into a more positive experience.

By encouraging positive reinforcement and support, we can help others to regulate their emotions effectively. Actively listening and validating others' emotions can help us to better manage interpersonal emotions. Using enthusiasm, optimism and encouragement may help to shape collective emotions in teams and groups. We can be mindful of how our emotions affect others and consciously cultivate positivity. And we can help others to manage their emotions by encouraging them to reflect on them before making important decisions.

A brief activity for cultivating emotions

Invite one or two family members, friends or colleagues to join you in this activity. Write down various emotions on pieces of paper, then fold them up and put them in a jar or a bowl. One by one, each participant then takes a piece of paper and conveys the emotion through non-verbal expressions. The other participants observe and try to guess the emotion expressed. Repeat this until each of the participants has expressed a number of emotions. Then reflect on the importance of expressing emotions, and how some of the emotions demonstrated can be managed in various situations and scenarios.

Personal vignette

Understanding and managing my emotions has enabled me to navigate many challenges in life. It has helped me to move forward with my goals, refocus my priorities and maintain positive relationships with people. To manage my emotions, I use strategies such as meditation, breathing exercises, journaling, physical exercise, and chanting mantra and spiritual prayers. Expressing my emotions to others always helps me in managing them.

Reflective questions

1. What are the best ways you use to understand your own emotions?
2. What are the best ways you can use to understand others' emotions?
3. How comfortable are you expressing your emotions authentically and openly in front of others?
4. How can you enhance your emotional expression?
5. How does expressing emotions affect your self-care and well-being?
6. What ways have helped you in the past to manage your emotions?
7. How can you create a positive atmosphere in a group setting at home and work?
8. What did you learn from Aitana' story?
9. What did you learn from Jonathan's story?

References and further reading

Fredrickson, B. L. (2000) Cultivating positive emotions to optimize health and well-being. *Prevention & Treatment*, 3(1), 1a.

Fredrickson, B. L. (2001) The role of positive emotions in positive psychology: The broaden-and-build theory of positive emotions. *American Psychologist*, 56(3), 218-226.

Ghosh, O., & Raj, M. S. S. (2025) The vital role of emotions in health decision-making. In: *Behavioral Economics and Neuroeconomics of Health and Healthcare* (pp. 299–332). IGI Global.

Goleman, D. (1995) *Emotional Intelligence: Why it can matter more than IQ*. Bantam Books.

Hatfield, E., Cacioppo, J., & Rapson, R. L. (1994) *Emotional Contagion*. New York: Cambridge University Press.

Kennedy-Moore, E., & Watson, J. C. (2001) *Expressing Emotion: Myths, realities, and therapeutic strategies*. Guilford Press.

Kok, B. E., Coffey, K. A., Cohn, M. A., Catalino, L. I., Vacharkulksemsuk, T., Algoe, S. B., ... & Fredrickson, B. L. (2013) How positive emotions build physical health: Perceived positive social connections account for the upward spiral between positive emotions and vagal tone. *Psychological Science*, 24(7), 1123-1132.

Pennebaker, J. W. (2012) *Opening Up: The healing power of expressing emotions*. Guilford Press.

Quoidbach, J., Berry, E. V., Hansenne, M., & Mikolajczak, M. (2010) Positive emotion regulation and well-being: Comparing the impact of eight savoring and dampening strategies. *Personality and Individual Differences*, 49(5), 368-373.

Rimé, B. (2009) Emotion elicits the social sharing of emotion: Theory and empirical review. *Emotion Review*, 1(1), 60-85.

Solomon, R. C. (2007) *True To Our Feelings*: What our emotions are really telling us. Oxford University Press.

Warnick, B. J., Davis, B. C., Allison, T. H., & Anglin, A. H. (2021) Express yourself: Facial expression of happiness, anger, fear, and sadness in funding pitches. *Journal of Business Venturing*, 36(4), 106109.

Zaki, J., & Ochsner, K. (2011) The cognitive neuroscience of sharing and understanding others' emotions. In: J. Decety (Ed) *Empathy: From bench to bedside*. MIT Press.

Chapter 6:

Forgiveness

"Forgive others, not because they deserve forgiveness, but because you deserve peace."

Jonathan Lockwood Huie

Forgiveness is letting go of feelings of anger or resentment towards people who hurt us. This is a transformative act that can bring us healing and inner peace. Forgiveness lets us break free from the shackles of resentment, allowing us to embrace the fullness of life with an open heart and mind. According to Thompson *et al*, forgiveness frees us from a negative attachment to the source that has transgressed against us.[20] The source of transgression or the target of forgiveness may be another person, oneself, or a situation that is viewed as out of one's control.

The act of forgiveness primarily means a reduced desire to avoid, harm or seek revenge toward a person. However, it also encompasses an increased desire to act positively toward them. Robert Enright defined forgiveness as *'a willingness to abandon one's right to resentment, negative judgement, and indifferent behaviour toward one who unjustly hurt us, while fostering the undeserved qualities of compassion, generosity, and even love towards him or her'.*[21]

Forgiveness is often seen as a gift we give to others, but in truth it is a profound act of self-liberation. Holding onto resentment weighs heavily on our hearts, while choosing to forgive, even in the face of betrayal, allows us to reclaim our peace and move forward with grace.

> **Have you forgiven someone at some point in your life? If yes, congratulations! If not, would you like to do it now? Here is an inspiring story about forgiveness from Marcia Reynolds:**
>
> *I grew up with my father telling me that the land he ran his business on had been bought personally in my mother's name, so no matter what happened to his wealth, the property would be our inheritance. There were four children, and we would each get equal shares.*
>
> *My mother passed away ten years after my father's death. She had remarried a retired man with little available cash. Five years after my father's death, her mind quickly deteriorated. When she died, she hadn't spoken a word in two years and could not get around without assistance. Much of the cash my father left to her she needed to spend for her own care and to care for her husband. Fortunately, the land had not been sold.*

---

20 Thompson *et al.*, 2005
21 Enright, Freedman & Rique, 1998

After my mother passed, a lawyer informed us that she had changed her will before she lost full faculty of her mind. My younger brother inherited all that was left of my father's estate, leaving nothing for me and my older siblings. My brother sold my father's business, including the land. He told me there were so many bills my father had racked up over the years, he used the money to pay off debts. Feeling cheated, I stopped speaking to him. He had deceived my mother and screwed my father and siblings. I could never forgive him for being so evil. Worse, I could not bear the thought of him caring so little about me.

A year later, I had dinner with an old friend who knew my family. I told him about my brother's actions. He replied, "Didn't you know your brother was a gambler?" My anger softened. The behaviour of an addict was something I understood; I had been addicted to drugs for years. And the perspective that he wasn't intent on hurting me, that he was under the control of his addiction, liberated me from my resentment.

That same day, a friend sent me an article about rape victims coping with their trauma through forgiveness. They did not forgive the act, but they learned to forgive the human, at least a little. I promised myself that I would work to forgive my brother as he struggled with addiction. As miracles would have it, I ran into him that day. He quickly invited me to his home to take the boxes of my mother's possessions he had saved for me. He never said it, but looking into his eyes, I sensed he was sorry.

I worked with a therapist that year to fully forgive my brother and focus on being grateful for the life I had created. I didn't need the money. I needed peace of mind.

Slowly but surely, I was able to love my brother again.

Marcia's story reminds us that forgiveness is not about excusing the past but freeing ourselves from its hold. By understanding her brother's struggles, Marcia found peace and rebuilt their relationship. Forgiveness takes courage and empathy, but it paves the way for healing and happiness. As you reflect on her story, consider what you might gain by letting go of resentment.

Forgiveness and happiness

Forgiveness facilitates emotional healing, reduces stress and fosters overall well-being. It frees us from the burden of negative emotions, which leads to better psychological and physical health. The release of negative emotions makes room for more positive emotions in our lives. Forgiveness reduces stress, anxiety and depressive symptoms, it repairs damaged relationships, and it improves relationships between people. Forgiving oneself and others enhances our self-esteem, hope, resilience and optimism, leading to enhanced psychological well-being and happiness. Forgiveness allows us to align with our true values and engage in purposeful behaviours, resulting in a more fulfilling life.

Scientific evidence

The interpersonal theory of forgiveness by Enright *et al* suggests that forgiveness leads to the restoration of healthy relationships among people, resulting in enhanced happiness.[22] According to this theory, by confronting and processing their feelings of hurt, individuals can find the way to emotional healing and reconciliation. Dispositional forgiveness theory by Thompson *et al* suggests that people with a higher propensity to forgive others experience less stress and better mental health.[23] And broaden-and-build theory argues that forgiveness may lead to the generation of positive emotions, leading to better health and fulfilment.

A recent meta-analysis review of eighty-three studies involving a total of almost forty thousand participants found that people who are able to forgive more easily had higher subjective well-being, greater life satisfaction, more positive emotions, and fewer negative emotions.[24] It was also found that forgiveness was closely related to both short- and long-term happiness. Earlier research has also provided longitudinal evidence showing that greater forgiveness is associated with less stress and, in turn, better mental health.[25]

---

22   Enright, Freedman & Rique, 1998
23   Thompson *et al.*, 2005
24   Gao, Li & Bai, 2022
25   Toussaint, Shields & Slavich, 2016

Personal vignette

In India, the idea of forgiving and forgetting is quite prominent in many communities, and many individuals forgive others and readily move forward. People have forgiven me for past mistakes I have made, and this has been motivational as well as bringing a sense of relief. I have seen family and colleagues reach out to others for forgiveness, and it was always a win-win for both parties. When I forgive other people, it brings me happiness and peace.

Cultivating forgiveness

Understanding the benefits of forgiveness can motivate you to begin the process. A realistic, undistorted appraisal of an event and the harm it caused may offer encouragement. Try to understand the challenges and circumstances of people who wronged you, as this is likely to make it easier to forgive them. According to the Tangney model of forgiveness, the giving up of negative emotions is the crux of the forgiving process.

If the person you need to forgive is yourself, try to reframe the narrative of what wrong you did to yourself. Focus on learning from the experience. You may wish to seek help from family, friends or professionals. Remain committed and be patient – these are the two key steps towards achieving the emotional release that forgiveness can bring. We need to realize that, when we forgive, it is we ourselves who reap the true rewards of peace and fulfilment.

A brief activity for cultivating forgiveness

Invite a small group of friends or colleagues to perform a role play on forgiveness. Create some hypothetical situations in which someone has wronged another person. Write these situations on separate pieces of paper, then fold them and put them in a jar or a bowl. Each group member then takes a random piece of paper and enacts the forgiving process. Members who don't wish to enact may engage in sketching or other activities based on their interests. Other members observe and give feedback on the process. The group then closes the session with a general discussion about the benefits of forgiving others and oneself.

Reflective questions

1. What would be the benefits if you were to forgive someone who did you wrong?

2. What emotions did you feel when you were forgiven for something you did wrong?

3. What emotions do you feel when you think of forgiving someone?

4. What steps can help you to cultivate a more forgiving attitude?

5. What steps can you take right now towards forgive someone?

6. What did you learn from Marcia's story?

References and further reading

Akhtar, S., Dolan, A., & Barlow, J. (2017) Understanding the relationship between state forgiveness and psychological wellbeing: A qualitative study. *Journal of Religion and Health*, 56, 450-463.

American Psychological Association. (2017) Forgiveness can improve mental and physical health. *Monitor on Psychology*. Available at: www.apa.org/monitor/2017/01/ce-corner?utm (accessed April 2025).

Booker, J. A., & Perlin, J. D. (2021) Using multiple character strengths to inform young adults' self-compassion: The potential of hope and forgiveness. *The Journal of Positive Psychology*, 16(3), 379-389.

Enright, R. D. (2019) Forgiveness is a choice: A step-by-step process for resolving anger and restoring hope. American Psychological Association.

Enright, R. D., Freedman, S., & Rique, J. (1998) The psychology of interpersonal forgiveness. In: R. D. Enright & J. North (Eds.) *Exploring Forgiveness* (pp. 46–63). Madison: University of Wisconsin Press.

Fredrickson, B. L. (2001) The role of positive emotions in positive psychology: The broaden-and-build theory of positive emotions. *American Psychologist*, 56(3), 218-226.

Gao, F., Li, Y., & Bai, X. (2022) Forgiveness and subjective well-being: A meta-analysis review. *Personality and Individual Differences*, 186, 111350.

Kaya, F., & Odacı, H. (2024) Subjective well-being: self-forgiveness, coping self-efficacy, mindfulness, and the role of resilience? *British Journal of Guidance & Counselling*, 52(4), 628-644.

McCullough, M. E. (2000) Forgiveness as human strength: Theory, measurement, and links to well-being. *Journal of Social and Clinical Psychology*, 19(1), 43-55.

Menahem, S., & Love, M. (2013) Forgiveness in psychotherapy: The key to healing. *Journal of Clinical Psychology*, 69(8), 829-835.

Parveen, U., & Pal, R. (2024) The impact of forgiveness in emotional regulation and resilience in the face of adversity among young adults. *International Journal for Multidisciplinary Research*, 6(2).

Pillai, S. (2021) Attachment Injury-Related Responses from the Offending Partner and Forgiveness in Romantic Relationships. University of Nebraska. Available at: https://digitalcommons.unl.edu/cgi/viewcontent.cgi?article = 1398&context = cehsdiss (accessed April 2025).

Thompson, L. Y., Snyder, C. R., Hoffman, L., Michael, S. T., Rasmussen, H. N., Billings, L. S., ... & Roberts, D. E. (2005) Dispositional forgiveness of self, others, and situations. *Journal of Personality*, 73(2), 313-360.

Tirrell, J. M. (2024) On forgiveness and character development: Description, explanation, and optimization. In: *The Routledge International Handbook of Multidisciplinary Perspectives on Character Development, Volume I* (pp. 439-458). Routledge.

Tiwari, G. K., Pandey, R., Parihar, P., & Rai, P. K. (2023) Self-forgiveness and human flourishing: understanding the mediating role of self-esteem. *Mental Health, Religion & Culture*, 26(5), 418-430.

Toussaint, L. L., Shields, G. S., & Slavich, G. M. (2016) Forgiveness, stress, and health: A 5-week dynamic parallel process study. *Annals of Behavioral Medicine*, 50(5), 727-735.

Weinberg, M., Altshuler, A., & Soffer, M. (2023) Relationships between mastery, forgiveness, optimism, and resilience, and PTSD and anxiety during the COVID-19 pandemic. *Psychology, Health & Medicine*, 28(9), 2537-2547.

G

Chapter 7:
Gratitude

"Gratitude is the fairest blossom which springs from the soul, and the heart of man. It is the secret of happiness hidden in plain sight."

Robert Ingersoll

Gratitude is appreciating and being thankful for the actions of another person. It is recognizing that you have received a positive outcome from another individual, who behaved in a manner that involved a measure of personal cost or sacrifice to them, was valuable to you, and was freely and intentionally given. The expression of gratitude may range from a polite 'thank you' in everyday life, to an appreciation and thankfulness for life itself.

In their book *Ikigai*, Héctor García and Francesc Miralles recommend that spending a moment each day giving thanks can grow our 'stockpile' of happiness.[26] Expressing gratitude toward other people reinforces our emotional connection with them and enriches the relationship between us. Being grateful is associated with many positive health benefits and improved well-being. Ultimately, it is through gratitude that we find lasting happiness – not in perfect circumstances, but in the value we place on our journey and the moments that shape it.

> **Here is an inspiring story from Fabiana Memmolo, who found that persistence and gratitude were the keys that unlocked peace, purpose and happiness:**
>
> *My life journey has been tumultuous – marked by personal storms, painful battles and numerous setbacks. For over half my life, I felt trapped in a cycle of unsuitability and misery, consumed by pain and anger. Family losses and professional failures weighed heavily on me; for years, I moved from one place to another, convinced that the next destination would bring the fulfilment and joy I longed for. Yet each new beginning left me grappling with the same restlessness, unable to find my place in the world and fully express my talents.*
>
> *Embracing positive psychology principles and cultivating a mindset of gratitude has helped me become a better person. Gratitude has been a transformative force in my life, teaching me resilience and revealing my ability to thrive despite adversity. The turning point came during the COVID-19 pandemic, a time of global uncertainty that intensified my fears. Amid the isolation and anxiety, I took part in an exercise focused on gratitude, mindfulness and appreciation, based on Deepak Chopra's principles. The exercise, organized by a group of friends, initially seemed like a minor commitment. However, it quickly turned into a profound moment of self-discovery.*

---

26   García & Miralles, 2017

Each day, I was encouraged to reflect on the positive aspects of my life and recognize the value and meaning in what I had created so far. Initially, overcoming feelings of helplessness was challenging. The sacrifices I made – leaving my home country, facing setbacks, and working tirelessly toward my dreams – felt like they might be in vain. However, the daily practice of gratitude shifted my perspective. Instead of fixating on what I hadn't yet achieved, I began to appreciate the foundation I had established. I saw how far I had come: I had my dream job as an executive coach, advanced my knowledge in academic research at a reputable institution in the UK, enhanced my skills, pursued graduate education in psychology, and demonstrated resilience through every challenge.

This realization gave me the strength to transform my helplessness – not in defeat, but in gratitude and compassion. I learned to trust that my sacrifices were not in vain, even if my progress wasn't immediately visible. Gratitude helped me recognize the abundance in my life: the love from friends and family who supported me, the comfort of a warm home, and the privilege of good health. It reminded me that the journey is meaningful, regardless of the outcome.

Over time, my gratitude practice became a tool for reframing adversity. While the pandemic was devastating, it also created space for introspection. It taught me to appreciate the small joys I once overlooked and trust the growth process, even when the path felt uncertain. I began to find meaning in success and the effort and perseverance that brought me to this point.

Gratitude deepened my appreciation for opportunities I had once taken for granted. I am profoundly grateful to have been born in a country that upholds human rights and values freedom of movement, providing me with safety and the flexibility to explore opportunities abroad when my professional life at home felt unfulfilling. Among those opportunities, I am incredibly thankful for the chance to live in the United States, where I achieved my lifelong dream of earning a PhD – a goal that once seemed beyond reach.

Reflecting on this privilege during one of the most challenging periods of my life gave me a renewed sense of purpose and stability, reminding me that even in moments of uncertainty, the foundations I've built hold great value and promise.

Happiness, I've learned, isn't found in a perfect place or an ideal moment. It's cultivated through gratitude – by embracing the value of what we already have and finding meaning in the journey itself. The pandemic taught me that light could be found in self-reflection, connection and resilience, even amid the darkness. Through gratitude, I have discovered a lasting sense of peace and purpose that continues to guide me toward my dreams and aspirations.

Gratitude is much more than simply saying 'thank you' – it has the power to transform adversity into growth. Fabiana found that embracing gratitude during challenging times, particularly through the turbulence of the COVID-19 pandemic, led to a profound shift in perspective. Her story highlights how gratitude can enhance well-being and deepen our connection both to ourselves and to the world around us.

Gratitude can be a powerful source of resilience, especially in challenging times. Mongezi Makhalima shares how gratitude became a guiding force during a difficult period:

Growing up in a country like South Africa during Apartheid, many people had a good reason to walk around angry, sad or just annoyed. And many did. But I have on many occasions been accused of optimism. Some have even experienced annoyance at it.

I always say that I had the privilege of being raised by my grandmother, who seemed to have buckets of resilience hidden in the house – especially as I reflect back to my childhood and realize things I took for granted, like the fact that she supported an extended family of fifteen in a small four-roomed house on her domestic salary.

She complained, yes, when we children were naughty or uncooperative, but never to the point where she made us feel like a burden. I never really reflected on this and I took its effect on me for granted – until the pandemic, where, during a very difficult period, I unconsciously tapped into this spirit of resilience to continue serving as a therapist and coach others who needed psychosocial support when death was in every supervision class and group session.

My key tool, I noticed, was a grounded sense of gratitude. I found that each morning I woke up not only grateful to be alive, but also feeling that everything I had been prepared for all my life was leading up to this particular moment. I felt that I was truly serving the world in a way that was fully aligned and unambiguous. It was the first time ever that I understood, honestly, the concept of gratitude. It was more than a thank you – it was more like a conscious acknowledgement of just being, connected and in service of something larger than myself.

Even today, I'm grateful for having that as an anchor moment. Because now, if I ever need to remember gratitude, all I have to do is think back to that moment. And it also taught me that gratitude is a huge source of resilience. What a gift!

In the face of adversity, gratitude becomes more than just a feeling – it transforms into an anchor that sustains us, a guiding force offering strength and clarity when we need it most. Mongezi's journey shows us that gratitude is not only about appreciating what we have, but also about recognizing the inner strength it cultivates. As Mongezi continues to navigate life's challenges, he carries forward the lesson that gratitude is not just a reaction; it is a choice, a practice, and a profound source of resilience. And for that, he is forever grateful.

Gratitude and happiness

Gratitude has profound effects on our well-being. Practicing gratitude encourages self-reflection, which affects personal growth, purpose and meaning in life. Regularly expressing gratitude reduces negative emotions like stress, anxiety and depression, and enhances mental health.

Expressing gratitude is associated with better physical health, too, including a strengthened immune system, better sleep and lower blood pressure. Individuals with a greater propensity to express gratitude have more positive emotions and a more positive outlook on life, all of which leads to enhanced well-being, life satisfaction and overall happiness.

The practice of gratitude may also help relationships to develop. Expressing gratitude reduces interpersonal mistreatment and strengthens interpersonal relationships, leading to higher happiness and life satisfaction. Individuals who regularly express gratitude receive greater social support from others, leading to improved well-being for all concerned. When we start noticing good qualities in others and start expressing gratitude to them, our relationship with them starts improving, even in difficult relationships, which contributes to happiness.

Scientific evidence

According to Michael McCullough and Robert Emmons, grateful people may be prone to positive emotions and subjective well-being.[27] A disposition toward gratitude is rooted in a basic tendency to experience positive emotions and subjective well-being. Expressing gratitude increases positive emotions, and therefore gratitude as a positive emotion can contribute to the upward spiral of well-being described in the broaden-and-build theory of positive emotions. Thus, expressing gratitude may help to build psychological and social resources, supporting better health and fulfilment. McCullough and Emmons also suggest that seeing oneself as the beneficiary of other people's generosity may lead one to feel affirmed, esteemed and valued, which can boost self-esteem and perceived social support, leading to greater fulfilment.

In his book *Think Like a Monk*, Jay Shetty emphasizes that gratitude can help us 'overcome the bitterness and pain that we all carry with us'.[28] According to Shetty, '… when you are present in gratitude, you can't be anywhere else'. Feeling simultaneously jealous and grateful may

---

27 McCullough, Emmons & Tsang, 2002
28 Shetty, 2020

seem difficult to do; Shetty quotes UCLA neuroscientist Alex Korb, who explains that: 'Once you start seeing things to be grateful for, your brain starts looking for more things to be grateful for.'

In a study by Emmons and McCullough, people with neuromuscular conditions were randomly assigned to either a gratitude group or a control group.[29] Participants assigned to the gratitude group were instructed to think and write down up to five things in their life that they were grateful for, and to do this for ten weeks. The results of the study showed that participants in the gratitude group were more optimistic, more energetic, more connected to other people, and more likely to have restful sleep.

A meta-analytic review of independent samples involving more than one hundred thousand participants found that gratitude positively correlated with subjective and psychological well-being.[30] In a recent Japanese study, gratitude was strongly associated with psychological well-being dimensions such as personal growth, positive relations with others and having purpose in life.[31] All these indicators contribute to enhanced happiness and well-being.

Personal vignette

I took part in a workshop on emotional intelligence and leadership led by Professor Richard Boyatzis. He asked all participants to think of three people who had helped us become what we were. We had to write down the words, actions or behaviours expressed by those people, as well as the feelings we had while recalling these things. Most participants felt positive emotions. I was inspired and filled with energy, and I have since used the activity many times myself.

Cultivating gratitude

We can cultivate gratitude simply by expressing it to others in an active way. Express gratitude verbally, send thank-you notes or perform small acts of kindness. Keep a gratitude journal and regularly write

29   Emmons & McCullough, 2003
30   Portocarrero, Gonzalez & Ekema-Agbaw, 2020
31   Nama & Yamagishi, 2024

down positive things other people do for you. Set aside time, daily or weekly, to reflect on the positive moments, people or processes that make you feel grateful. Develop a habit of thanking people as soon as possible after receiving help from them. Notice the positive feelings you have while recalling the positive acts done by others for you. The acknowledgement of those positive feelings can significantly increase your sense of gratitude over time.

The practice of writing letters of gratitude can cultivate an attitude of thankfulness. Martin Seligman, the father of positive psychology, strongly advocates for writing letters of gratitude to people who have impacted your life significantly, visiting those individuals, and reading the letter out loud in front of them. In my own Science of Happiness class, I ask students to write a letter of gratitude to someone. When I ask them how they felt while writing the letter and afterwards, many of them share that the activity was deeply fulfilling and they felt very positive. Some shared that, as they were writing, they realized for the first time how many positive things the person had done for them. This was a fulfilling and inspiring experience. All of them promised to read out their letters to the people to whom they had been written.

Looking for the silver lining in difficult situations is a good way to make expressing gratitude part of our everyday mindset. Establishing rituals may help us to cultivate the habit. For example, in India, many people touch the earth after waking and say: 'Thank you, Mother Earth'. Sikhs say *Waheguru Tera Lakh-Lakh Shukar Hai* – which means 'God, I thank you a hundred thousand times' – many times each day. All over the world, there are rituals and traditions that emphasize the importance of expressing gratitude and suggest ways for doing so. Think of specific times when you would like to express your gratitude to God, the Earth, mother nature, your own body or whoever you feel is deserving of it. Whatever resonates with you, follow that instinct and find ways to express gratitude that are comfortable for you.

A brief activity for cultivating gratitude

Have a jar or a transparent container for this activity in your home or office. Whenever you feel grateful for something, write it on a piece of paper, fold it and put it in the jar. Set time aside once a month or on special occasions to empty the jar and read all the notes. Share your feelings with family and friends. A similar activity, and a variation on the Three Good Things technique, is to take a few minutes at the end of each day to list three things for which you are grateful and meditate on the gift inherent in each. Write a phrase such as I am grateful to _____ because _____. In the first blank, list the person, event, or thing for which you are grateful, and in the second, state the reasons. Continue the activity at least for three weeks. Discuss the effects with a family member or friends after a period of one week.[32]

Reflective questions

1. Think of a person who has made a positive impact on you recently.

2. What was that impact?

3. How did you feel when you expressed gratitude to someone?

4. How can you incorporate gratitude into your daily life?

5. What would be the impact on you if you lived your life with profound gratitude?

6. What did you learn from Fabiana's story?

7. What did you learn from Mongezi's story?

References and further reading

Basit, A., Ali, R., Rahman, S., & Shah, A. A. (2024) Exploring how the Practice of Gratitude can Strengthen Interpersonal Relationships, Enhance Mental Well-being, Foster Emotional Resilience, and Promote greater Social Connectedness and Cooperation. *Review of Education, Administration & Law*, 7(4), 427-441.

Boggiss A. L., Consedine N. S., Brenton-Peters J. M., Hofman P.L., Serlachius A.S. (2020) A systematic review of gratitude interventions: Effects on physical health and health behaviors. *J Psychosom Res*. https://doi.org/10.1016/j. jpsychores.2020.110165.

Borawski, D. (2022) When you are lonely, look inside yourself: the moderating role of reflection in the relationship between loneliness and meaning in life. *Personality and Individual Differences*, 194, 111662.

Emmons, R. A., & McCullough, M. E. (2003) Counting blessings versus burdens: an experimental investigation of gratitude and subjective well-being in daily life. *Journal of Personality and Social Psychology*, 84(2), 377-389.

Fekete, E. M., & Deichert, N. T. (2022) A brief gratitude writing intervention decreased stress and negative affect during the COVID-19 pandemic. *Journal of Happiness Studies*, 23(6), 2427-2448.

---

32   Adapted from Emmons, R. A., & McCullough, M. E. (2003) Counting blessings versus burdens: an experimental investigation of gratitude and subjective well-being in daily life. *Journal of Personality and Social Psychology*, 84(2), 377-389

Fredrickson, B. L. (2004). Gratitude, like other positive emotions, broadens and builds. In: R. A. Emmons & M. E. McCullough (Eds.) *The Psychology of Gratitude* (pp. 145–166). Oxford University Press.

García, H., & Miralles, F. (2017) *Ikigai: The Japanese secret to a long and happy life.* Penguin.

Hazlett, L. I., Moieni, M., Irwin, M. R., Haltom, K. E. B., Jevtic, I., Meyer, M. L., ... & Eisenberger, N. I. (2021) Exploring neural mechanisms of the health benefits of gratitude in women: A randomized controlled trial. *Brain, Behavior, and Immunity*, 95, 444-453.

Jackowska, M., Brown, J., Ronaldson, A., & Steptoe, A. (2016) The impact of a brief gratitude intervention on subjective well-being, biology and sleep. *Journal of health psychology*, 21(10), 2207-2217.

Ko, H., Kim, S., & Kim, E. (2021) Nursing students' experiences of gratitude journaling during the COVID-19 pandemic. *Healthcare*, 9(11), 1473.

Kross, E., Ong, M., & Ayduk, O. (2023) Self-reflection at work: Why it matters and how to harness its potential and avoid its pitfalls. *Annual Review of Organizational Psychology and Organizational Behavior*, 10(1), 441-464.

Locklear, L. R., Taylor, S. G., & Ambrose, M. L. (2021) How a gratitude intervention influences workplace mistreatment: A multiple mediation model. *Journal of Applied Psychology*, 106(9), 1314.

McCullough, M. E., Emmons, R. A., & Tsang, J. A. (2002) The grateful disposition: a conceptual and empirical topography. *Journal of Personality and Social Psychology*, 82(1), 112-127.

Nawa, N. E., & Yamagishi, N. (2024) Distinct associations between gratitude, self-esteem, and optimism with subjective and psychological well-being among Japanese individuals. *BMC Psychology*, 12(1), 130.

Passmore, J., & Oades, L. G. (2016) Positive psychology techniques – gratitude. *Coaching Psychologist*, 12(1), 34–35.

Portocarrero, F. F., Gonzalez, K., & Ekema-Agbaw, M. (2020) A meta-analytic review of the relationship between dispositional gratitude and well-being. *Personality and Individual Differences*, 164, 110101.

Shetty, J. (2020) *Think Like a Monk: Train your mind for peace and purpose every day.* Simon & Schuster.

Waters, L., Algoe, S. B., Dutton, J., Emmons, R., Fredrickson, B. L., Heaphy, E., ... & Steger, M. (2022) Positive psychology in a pandemic: Buffering, bolstering, and building mental health. *The Journal of Positive Psychology*, 17(3), 303-323.

Waters, L., Algoe, S. B., Dutton, J., Emmons, R., Fredrickson, B. L., Heaphy, E., ... & Steger, M. (2022) Positive psychology in a pandemic: Buffering, bolstering, and building mental health. *The Journal of Positive Psychology*, 17(3), 303-323.

You, S., Lee, J., & Lee, Y. (2022) Relationships between gratitude, social support, and prosocial and problem behaviors. *Current Psychology*, 41(5), 2646-2653.

H

Chapter 8:
Helping

"If you want happiness for an hour, take a nap.
If you want happiness for a day, go fishing.
If you want happiness for a year, inherit a fortune.
If you want happiness for a lifetime, help someone."

Chinese proverb

Helping is a natural expression of human kindness and a powerful source of happiness and satisfaction. One of the most reaffirming moments of the past two decades was the Dalai Lama's statement in 2009 that humans not only engage in generous behaviour; we also appear to derive pleasure from doing so. Helping others is beneficial both for those who being helped and for those doing the helping. It enhances the well-being of both parties. Helping others enhances compassion, enriches social relationships, and builds resilient communities and an equitable society at large. One of the best ways to make yourself happy is to make other people happy. When we act prosocially, we experience different aspects of well-being every day.

Helping is a natural expression of human kindness – an act of offering support, care or encouragement to others. It reflects our shared humanity and our innate capacity to uplift one another. Helping others depends on understanding, compassion and a sense of social responsibility. It can take many forms, such as providing objects/resources, empathizing with other people, encouraging others, dedicating time and energy, sharing knowledge and advocating for equality and human rights.

Helping and happiness

Helping may lead to positive differences in others' lives, generating a sense of fulfilment and satisfaction for the helper. Helping others boosts self-esteem by eliciting positive emotions, and it enhances interpersonal relationships which increases our psychological well-being. Engaging in acts of kindness reduces negative emotions such as stress and anxiety, improving our psychological health. And helping also has a positive impact on physical health – engaging in helping behaviour following a stressor can help mitigate physiological stress responses, leading to greater downregulation of heart rate, diastolic blood pressure, and mean arterial pressure.

A very simple reason to help someone is that it feels good. Telling someone they look great and then seeing their bashful smile gives a giddy, joyous feeling. Even indirect gratification such as when we help someone anonymously by giving a tip can promote psychological changes that give happiness. Hence, people sometimes help others simply because they want to feel good. Their mood will be more positive, and they will have a more optimistic approach towards life, which will help offset any negative feelings and emotions.

Helping also enhances happiness by facilitating the creation and development of new bonds that strengthen our social well-being. When we are helping others, it redirects our minds towards them and away from our own worries and doubts, and this can significantly reduce stress and anxiety. Sometimes, simply seeing others being happy is enough to put a smile on our own faces.

Acts of kindness benefit others but also bring deep fulfilment for us. Ian Day shares how helping others has shaped his life and career, creating ripples of impact and lasting joy:

If I look back over my life and career and think about what has made me happy, it is always related to helping others. When I reflect on this, I think about Maslow's hierarchy of needs, and the highest-level being self-actualization. I feel happy when I have had the opportunity to help other people, and so living my purpose, achieving my potential with meaning.

I have worked as a leadership coach for over twenty years, and during that time I have been humbled as I have helped people become more fulfilled, satisfied and motivated. This sense of satisfaction and fulfilment encouraged me to seek my current job as Associate Professor for the postgraduate coaching qualifications at a top UK university. In this role, I can develop coaches and also work to enhance the quality of coaching as a profession. It's a huge pleasure to hear about the impact the courses have had on participants, how it has helped them in their lives and careers in so many different ways. This provides a huge sense of satisfaction and happiness.

When I think about this, a metaphor comes to mind – that of dropping a pebble into a pond of water. As the pebble enters the water, it creates ripples which radiate outwards, impacting a wide area of the pond. This strikes me as the way that my leadership coaching and coach development courses radiate outwards to help individuals, organizations and society as a whole. This is hugely satisfying and provides a huge sense of happiness and fulfilment as I have been able to help so many people in this way for so many years.

Ian reminds us that helping others is not just an act of kindness – it is a path to lasting fulfilment. Each small act of support creates ripples, touching lives in ways we may never fully see. When we help others to grow, we grow too, finding meaning and happiness along the way.

Scientific evidence

Our happiness is often boosted more by providing support to other people than by receiving support ourselves, and studies have shown that there is a positive association between helping and happiness. A systematic review and meta-analysis were conducted to assess the effect of acts of kindness on the well-being of the person being kind.[33] Twenty-seven experimental studies were included in this review, which found that kindness had a positive effect on well-being. Another study found that volunteering and helping others was correlated with increases in overall life satisfaction, positive affect and reduced depression.[34]

Jonathan Passmore and Lindsay Oades have suggested that performing random acts of kindness may increase hope and self-regard, which can contribute to happiness.[35] According to Daniel Batson *et al*, having empathy for another person increases the likelihood of helping that person.[36] Humans, at times, are sufficiently moved by their empathies to help other people. As people engage in helping others with genuine concern for their well-being, it leads to increased happiness and satisfaction for them. Following social exchange theory, people also engage in helping others to get benefits in return. People who extend help to others may receive reciprocal help, gain social approval, or have enhanced relationships leading to greater happiness.[37]

In one recent study, the researchers investigated what can support people during the period of transition from becoming a teenager to starting university.[38] First-year students were recruited during the first

33   Curry *et al.*, 2018
34   Aknin *et al.*, 2019
35   Passmore & Oades, 2015
36   Batson, Ahmad & Lishner, 2009
37   Cropananzo & Mitchell, 2005
38   Cash, Aknin & Girme, 2024

two weeks of the fall semester over two consecutive years. The students' well-being levels were captured using seven validated scales. They were also assessed on a 47-item behavioural checklist (with 42 prosocial items) to assess whether and how often participants engaged in various forms of prosocial action. These actions included baking treats and dropping them off to friends, volunteering in the community, and helping people carry items. During the data analysis, it was found that participants reported greater happiness, thriving, flourishing, optimism and resilience, and lower anxiety and loneliness, in the weeks when they participated in more types of prosocial action than their personal average. The researchers therefore suggested that helping others could be a potentially useful route to well-being during life transitions.

Cultivating helping

Helping is not about grand gestures – it's about showing up in small ways, every day. Listen attentively whenever others share their concerns and develop a genuine understanding of their difficulties and problems. Offer your support and encouragement without being judgemental of their situations and capabilities. Find volunteering opportunities where you can contribute your time and energy. Provide tangible support for people who are less fortunate using the resources you have. Practice making small acts of kindness whenever you get an opportunity to do so. Offer compliments and smiles to brighten other people's days.

Lead by example and invite others to join you in your initiatives to help others. Helping someone to think big is one of the most generous gifts you can give. Words of enthusiasm and confidence from a friend can inspire people to tackle far more ambitious goals than they might consider on their own. Bringing people together can also be a great way to help people, which enhances everyone's happiness. If in doubt, ask another person how you could contribute to enhancing their happiness. Note, though, that it's important not to lose sight of self-care, so that you can avoid burnout and have enough energy to contribute to others' welfare.

Personal vignette

A friend was unable to fund his child's education, so I asked someone I knew to sponsor them. That person agreed, and has been continuously paying the child's school fees, books and transport for the last ten years. Though I didn't directly help the person, I am always happy to see that the child is getting a good education, thanks to my request. So, in this instance, simply encouraging someone else to help another person gave me happiness and fulfilment.

A brief activity for cultivating helping

When it comes starting out with a plan to help others, you don't need to make grand gestures. You can begin with small acts of kindness that fit easily into your daily routine. For example smile and greet people with warmth, hold the door open for someone, ask someone how their day is going, help an older person to carry groceries, or simply listen to someone. These small actions will brighten your day and the day of the person you're helping.

Reflective questions

1. What small act of kindness will you commit to today?
2. Reflect on a time when someone helped you. How did that impact you?
3. Reflect on a time when you helped someone. How did that impact you?
4. What motivates you to extend help to others?
5. How is helping others related to happiness?
6. What can you do to increase helping behaviour?
7. Who do you consider to be role models for helping others? What learning emerges for you when you think about them and their helping behaviour?
8. What did you learn from Ian's story?

References and further reading

Aknin, L. B., & Whillans, A. V. (2021) Helping and happiness: A review and guide for public policy. *Social Issues and Policy Review*, 15(1), 3-34.

Aknin, L. B., Whillans, A. V., Norton, M. I., & Dunn, E. W. (2019) Happiness and prosocial behavior: An evaluation of the evidence. In: J. F. Helliwell, R. Layard, & J. Sachs (Eds.), *World Happiness Report 2019* (pp. 67–86). Sustainable Development Solutions Network.

Batson, C. D. (1991) *The Altruism Question: Toward a social-psychological answer*. Hillsdale, NJ: Erlbaum

Batson, C. D., Ahmad, N., & Lishner, D. A. (2009) Empathy and altruism. In: S. J. Lopez & C. R. Snyder (Eds.) *The Oxford Handbook of Positive Psychology* (pp. 417–426). Oxford University Press.

Beeler-Duden, S., & Vaish, A. (2024) Feeling good and feeling thankful: The role of positive emotions in sustaining early prosocial behavior. In: M. D. Matthews & R. M. Lerner (Eds.) *The Routledge International Handbook of Multidisciplinary Perspectives on Character Development* (Vol. 1, pp. 587–610). Routledge.

Cash, T. A., Aknin, L. B., & Girme, Y. U. (2024) Everyday acts of kindness predict greater well-being during the transition to university. *Social and Personality Psychology Compass*, 18(6), e12972.

Cropanzano, R., & Mitchell, M. S. (2005) Social exchange theory: An interdisciplinary review. *Journal of management*, 31(6), 874-900.

Curry, O. S., Rowland, L. A., Van Lissa, C. J., Zlotowitz, S., McAlaney, J., & Whitehouse, H. (2018) Happy to help? A systematic review and meta-analysis of the effects of performing acts of kindness on the well-being of the actor. *Journal of Experimental Social Psychology*, 76, 320-329.

Fu, X., Padilla-Walker, L. M., & Brown, M. N. (2017) Longitudinal relations between adolescents' self-esteem and prosocial behavior toward strangers, friends and family. *Journal of Adolescence*, 57, 90-98.

Hui, B. P. (2022) Prosocial behavior and well-being: Shifting from the 'chicken and egg' to positive feedback loop. *Current Opinion in Psychology*, 44, 231-236.

Hui, B. P. H., Ng, J. C. K., Berzaghi, E., Cunningham-Amos, L. A., & Kogan, A. (2020) Rewards of kindness? A meta-analysis of the link between prosociality and well-being. *Psychological Bulletin*, 146(12), 1084–1116.

Lauri, M. A., & Calleja, S. S. (2019) Prosocial behaviour and psychological wellbeing. In: Vella, S., Falzon, R. & Azzopardi, A. (Eds) *Perspectives on Wellbeing* (pp. 46-62). Brill.

Lazar, L., & Eisenberger, N. I. (2022) The benefits of giving: Effects of prosocial behavior on recovery from stress. *Psychophysiology*, 59(2), e13954.

Pakaslahti, L., Karjalainen, A., & Keltikangas-Järvinen, L. (2002) Relationships between adolescent prosocial problem-solving strategies, prosocial behaviour, and social acceptance. *International Journal of Behavioral Development*, 26(2), 137-144.

Passmore, J., & Oades, L. (2015) Positive psychology coaching techniques: random acts of kindness, consistent acts of kindness & empathy. *The Coaching Psychologist*, 11(2), 90–92. https://doi.org/10.1002/9781119835714.ch49

Peak, R. M., & McGarty, C. (2024) HOPEFUL: Helping Others Promotes Engagement and Fulfillment. *European Review of Social Psychology*, 1-44.

Rubin, G. (2009) *The Happiness Project: Or, why I spent a year trying to sing in the morning, clean my closets, fight right, read Aristotle, and generally have more fun*. HarperCollins.

Shillington, K. J., Johnson, A. M., Mantler, T., & Irwin, J. D. (2021) Kindness as an intervention for student social interaction anxiety, affect, and mood: The KISS of kindness study. *International Journal of Applied Positive Psychology*, 6(1), 23-44.

I

Chapter 9:

Intentions

"Happiness is not something you postpone for the future; it is something you design for the present."

Jim Rohn

Intentions are the compass that guides us toward what truly matters in life. Without them, it's easy to feel overwhelmed and stuck in an endless cycle of demands and routines. Intentions are not just about what we want to do today – they are also about who we want to become tomorrow. They are conscious choices or purposes that sit behind our actions, thoughts or behaviours. They are ingrained in our desires, values, aspirations and beliefs, and they act as a guiding force that influences our decisions and behaviour.

Intentions are aligned with an individual's overarching goals and objectives. When we set our intentions, we engage in a thoughtful and conscious process of deciding what we want to create, in order to achieve the level of focus that will be required to succeed. This requires awareness of our thoughts, emotions and actions. And, in turn, our intentions can themselves shape our thoughts, emotions and actions. Happiness comes not from doing more, but in doing what matters most – with intention. When we live with positive intentions, we unconsciously inspire others around us – creating ripples of happiness in our families, workplaces and communities.

This inspiring account from Holly Andrews show how setting clear intentions can help us success in bringing focus, purpose and happiness to our lives:

I was chatting with a friend about how my to-do list was out of control. I was on a hamster wheel, which was getting faster and faster, and I desperately wanted to get off. She said "Ah! You're talking about spaciousness – room to breathe, room to think, room to just be."

This was a lightbulb moment for me. It was exactly what I wanted, I just couldn't articulate it. Around the same time, my colleague recommended the book '4000 Weeks'. The author Oliver Burkeman states that, in our finite time, we will never do all the things we want to do, so we might as well focus on what's really important to us and accept that we'll never do the rest.

> *From these insights, I created an intention for how I was going to spend my time, my life, from that point on. I was going to consciously create spaciousness for myself. I created a mind map of my priorities and identified what was most important. I consult it every time I'm getting overwhelmed and losing my spaciousness. It focuses me on what is important and stops me getting involved in things that don't matter to me. Sometimes, it means I decline exciting projects, or say no to social events that would be fun. But I do this because my intention is very clear: I want spaciousness. I don't want to be on that hamster wheel.*
>
> *Keeping that intention front and centre makes it much easier to keep my actions aligned with what really matters to me, and I am so much happier for it.*

Holly's story shows how clear intentions can transform our lives by helping us focus on what truly matters. Reflect on your own priorities and consider setting an intention that aligns with your values. A small step toward clarity can lead to a more joyful and purposeful life.

Intentions and happiness

Happiness is not a by-product of achieving goals, but a result of living each day with intention. When we set an intention, we are clear about what we want to achieve, reducing feelings of uncertainty and leading to a relaxed mind and greater satisfaction. When setting intentions, we reflect on our values and align our intentions with our purpose and aspirations, leading to greater fulfilment in life. Intentions inspire us to act, helping us achieve our goals and contributing to improved well-being. When we set intentions, we become more mindful of our emotions and thoughts, leading to greater self-awareness. Setting intentions encourages us to take ownership of our lives, leading to greater self-control. This increased self-control in turn enhances self-confidence and hope, which contributes to enhanced happiness and satisfaction.

Having the intention to enhance happiness will inspire us to find appropriate interventions to achieve that goal, and we will be more mindful of our experiences, which contributes to greater happiness. When we share our intention to boost our happiness with others, we might receive more support from them, which can help us. When we have intentions to enhance happiness, we notice more cues in the environment that add to our positive emotional states, again leading to enhanced happiness and well-being.

Scientific evidence

According to the theory of planned behaviour, intentions are the most significant predictor of behaviour. Many scientific studies have confirmed that intentions do indeed predict behaviour and outcomes. Peter Gollwitzer suggests that intentions work by eliciting situational cues that remind individuals to engage in desired behaviours at a subconscious level.[39] Locke and Latham's goal-setting theory suggests that intentions direct an individual to exert their efforts towards behavioural outcomes.[40] Such findings can be applied to the goal of achieving happiness.

In a piece of experimental research, Lyubomirsky *et al* found that having the intention to become happier positively predicts greater gains from engaging in happiness interventions.[41] Following mindfulness theory, when we set intentions mindfully, we remain attuned and alert to present moments, and this too may contribute to enhanced overall happiness.

Cultivating intentions

In his book *Atomic Habits*, James Clear emphasizes the importance of having implementation intentions, which are the plans you make in advance about when and where to act.[42] According to Clear, being specific about what you want and how you will achieve it helps you say no to things that derail your progress and try to pull you off course. Intentions, along with required actions, lead to higher rates of goal achievement. Setting intentions for happiness can help keep

---

39   Gollwitzer, 1999
40   Locke & Latham, 2002
41   Lyubormirsky *et al.*, 2011
42   Clear, 2018

you focused, while creating clear plans for what you'll do and when you'll do it supports consistent efforts to improve your happiness and well-being.

Whenever you feel there is a need to enhance your well-being, this should trigger the intention-setting process. Be clear about what aspects of your life you want to focus on, create and use positive affirmations, and assess their impact on intention setting. Set aside a specific time each day, or once a week, for intention setting. Share your intentions with your family members or friends so that they can support you and encourage you to exert greater efforts towards achieving your goals. Request someone to be your accountability partner, with responsibility for helping you to stay committed.

Happiness isn't about doing more – it's about doing what matters most. Instead of chasing busyness, we can design a life that aligns with our values and well-being. With clarity, strategic choices and a supportive community around us, we can discover that fulfilment comes not from doing everything, but from doing what truly matters to us.

From the outside, Pamela Larde's life appears to be a whirlwind of roles and responsibilities. Yet things aren't hectic or out of control; Pamela is an example of the power of intention:

People often ask me: "How do you do it all?" On the surface, my life looks incredibly full. I'm an entrepreneur, a college professor, a writer, a mother, and a professional football player. But I don't see myself as busy. I see myself as intentional. Everything I do is rooted in a conscious choice, a strategy, and a community that nurtures my vision. My ability to integrate multiple roles comes down to three key commitments:

1. A Clear Vision. At twenty-five, I made the decision to create a life where I could be my whole self. I wanted to build professional spaces that allowed people, especially parents, to fully embrace both their careers and their personal passions.

> *2. A Strategic Shift. In my early thirties, I transitioned from a traditional nine-to-five job into academia. Teaching at the graduate level gave me the flexibility to design a schedule that aligned with my goals and priorities. I didn't wait for balance to happen – I created it.*
>
> *3. A Nurturing Community. I surrounded myself with people who supported my vision and let go of relationships that drained my energy. Protecting my joy and well-being has been essential in sustaining this life.*
>
> *So, when people ask me how I do it all, my answer is simple – I don't do everything. I do what matters, with intention. I don't chase busyness. I move with purpose.*
>
> *Living with intention means doing what aligns with who you are.*

Pamela's story reminds us that happiness isn't about doing more; it's about acting with intention. When we make choices, protect our energy, and align our actions with our purpose, life feels meaningful and fulfilling. True happiness comes from doing what matters most.

Personal vignette

Intentions are the foundation for achieving our goals of enhanced happiness and well-being. As a coach, I have often observed that setting intentions leads coaches to take appropriate actions. Whenever I feel the need to enhance my well-being, I take conscious actions and make it happen. However, I have also learned that taking action on the basis of advice which is not compatible with my own values or beliefs will not enhance my happiness.

A brief activity for cultivating intentions

Find a quiet place where you have no distractions. Take a few deep breaths to calm your mind. Take a piece of paper and write down a specific intention for enhancing your happiness. Reflect and check whether this intention is aligned with your values, your beliefs and your overall life aspirations. Then, write down some actions that will help you fulfil your intention.

Reflective questions

1. What aspects of life do you want to focus on for enhancing happiness and satisfaction?

2. What intentions for enhancing happiness are aligned to your values, beliefs and aspirations?

3. What resources and support do you need to implement your happiness intentions?

4. How can your intentions contribute to the happiness of others?

5. What are the obstacles on the way and how can you overcome them?

6. What did you learn from Holly's story?

7. What did you learn from Pamela's story?

References and further reading

Ajzen, I. (1985) From intentions to action: A theory of planned behavior. In: J. Kuhl & J. Beckmann (Eds.) *Action-control: From cognition to behavior* (pp. 11–39). New York: Springer.

Brown, K. W., & Ryan, R. M. (2003) The benefits of being present: mindfulness and its role in psychological well-being. *Journal of Personality and Social Psychology*, 84(4), 822-848.

Clear, J. (2018) *Atomic Habits: An easy & proven way to build good habits & break bad* ones. Avery. New York, NY.

Duckworth, A. L., Milkman, K. L., & Laibson, D. (2018) Beyond Willpower: Strategies for reducing failures of self-control. *Psychological Science in the Public Interest*, 19(3), 102-129.

Gollwitzer, P. M. (1999) Implementation intentions: Strong effects of simple plans. *American Psychologist*, 54, 493–503

Gollwitzer, P. M., & Sheeran, P. (2006) Implementation intentions and goal achievement: A meta-analysis of effects and processes. *Advances in Experimental Social Psychology*, 38, 69-119.

Lama, D. (2009) *The Art of Happiness: A handbook for living*. Penguin.

Locke, E. A., & Latham, G. P. (2002) Building a practically useful theory of goal setting and task motivation: A 35-year odyssey. *American Psychologist*, 57, 705-717.

Lyubomirsky, S., Dickerhoof, R., Boehm, J. K., & Sheldon, K. M. (2011) Becoming happier takes both a will and a proper way: an experimental longitudinal intervention to boost well-being. *Emotion*, 11(2), 391-402.

Schippers, M. C., & Ziegler, N. (2019) Life crafting as a way to find purpose and meaning in life. *Frontiers in Psychology*, 10, 2778.

Sheldon, K. M., Ryan, R. M., Deci, E. L., & Kasser, T. (2004) The independent effects of goal contents and motives on well-being: It's both what you pursue and why you pursue it. *Personality and Social Psychology Bulletin*, 30(4), 475-486.

J

Chapter 10:
Journaling

"Journaling is like whispering to oneself and listening at the same time."

Mina Murray

Journaling is writing down personal thoughts, emotions, experiences and reflections, either on paper or in digital form. It is like holding a mirror to your inner world – reflecting the chaos, clarity and beauty within. It is normally done by writing whatever comes to mind rather than evaluating and planning in advance. Research suggests that journaling for three to four minutes can reduce stress and enhance happiness. It is sometimes helpful to have prompts to start with, and then to continue writing for at least a few minutes. People engage in journaling to express their emotions, concerns, thoughts, goals, stressful issues and positive experiences. It can be used to unpack confusion, express gratitude, organise tasks or simply for expressive writing.

- **Free writing:** Writing whatever comes to mind without filtering or judging. This form of journaling helps in unpacking confusion and accepting emotions.
- **Gratitude journaling:** Listing things you're grateful for. Helps to shift the focus from what is lacking to what is abundant.
- **Bullet journaling:** Combining task lists, goals and reflections to organize daily life. It helps in tracking progress towards goals and enables you to review habitual patterns.
- **Expressive writing:** Writing about emotional experiences to process trauma and heal emotionally.

Journaling and happiness

Journaling helps enhance happiness. Research participants have reported the positive impact of journaling on their overall well-being. It helps us express our concerns, and while we do so, the built-up stress around those issues gets reduced, leading to a more relaxed state of mind. After journaling, we get clarity of thought, which helps us to see the issues we face from new perspectives. We get more ideas to solve our problems and to achieve our goals. Journaling with gratitude for positive experiences enhances positive emotions and boosts happiness.

For many, journaling is a powerful tool to enhance happiness, particularly through practices like gratitude journaling. Many people use expressive journaling to process trauma and negative emotions. However, staying consistent can be a challenge. In *Atomic Habits* James Clear emphasizes that, through journaling, nearly everyone can benefit from getting thoughts out of their head and onto paper. But many people give up after a few weeks because it feels like a chore.

He suggests that people seek ways of journaling that resonate with them – they can be creative, and they can continue to do it on a daily basis even if only for a short while.[43]

Journaling can be made enjoyable, effective and rewarding by approaching it in creative ways. Sam Isaacson blended technology with tradition to find his own unique solution:

I'm a coach, and I host a community of coaches experimenting with cutting-edge technology (the Coachtech Collective), so when there are opportunities for these worlds to collide, I have to make the most of them. I often find myself discussing the topic of a gratitude journal with my clients but have always found that I lack the discipline to do it myself. There's something about the fact that I can think it faster than writing it down that stops me from committing. What I really need is someone else to prod me every so often and tell me how good I've got it.

So I created a personalized AI cheerleader for myself. "His" name's Wilf – don't ask.

Every couple of weeks he reads through the gratitude journal I now keep, and he sends me a deeply personal email. In it, he reminds me of some of the things I've been grateful for. He points out recurring themes. He even makes a cheesy recommendation, and on one occasion surprised me by writing a poem! By turning my journal into a game that comes with a pleasant email every fortnight, I've taken a personal challenge and made it much more rewarding.

The poem wasn't very good. But it did bring a smile to my face, so what else can I ask for?

Sam's creative use of technology in journaling shows that making the practice enjoyable can enhance its impact on happiness. His approach reminds us that journaling is a personal experience, and that finding what works best for us can lead to improved well-being.

---

43   Clear, 2018

Scientific evidence

Tara Riddell *et al*, in a book chapter on healthy habits, suggest that adopting journaling may reduce burnout and anxiety, as well as enhancing happier mental states in physicians' personal and professional lives.[44] Karen Baikie and Kay Wilhelm conducted a review of the existing studies to synthesize findings on the emotional and physical health benefits of expressive writing.[45] They found that writing about traumatic, stressful or emotional events resulted in improvements in both physical and psychological health, in non-clinical and clinical populations. Participants who did so generally had significantly better physical and psychological outcomes compared with those who wrote about neutral topics. When we write about previous accomplishments, it may enhance our self-efficacy, which may contribute to higher happiness and well-being through greater efforts and positive coping approaches towards problems.

Reflective and emotional writing leads to better outcomes such as reduced anxiety and stress and better positive outcomes such as enhanced happiness and mental health. Journaling leads to positive mental states by giving us sharper mental clarity and making us better able to manage our emotions. Through self-reflection and goal setting, journaling helps us nurture a growth mindset, which in turn helps us adopt a more positive and proactive approach to challenges.

Here is a flowchart to explain how journaling enhances happiness:

Expression
⬇
Clarity
⬇
Insights
⬇
Action
⬇
Emotional Relief
⬇
Happiness

---

44   Riddell *et al.*, 2020
45   Baikie & Wilhelm, 2005

Cultivating journaling

Building a consistent practice of journaling for a few minutes every day can cultivate a good journaling practice. Doing it continuously for a few days will begin to show positive effects, which may motivate you to stay engaged. Joining or forming groups with people who journal regularly may inspire you to start journaling for different benefits. Knowing about different types of journaling may also provide ideas as to which type of journaling can be used in specific situations, leading to journaling becoming an increasingly large part of your self-care. Keeping a journal with you wherever you go also enhances opportunities to keep going at it. Having some prompts which can be used to start journaling may be helpful in enhancing your journaling practice, while adding visual elements may make it more creative and fun.

Here is a three-step framework for cultivating journaling:

Start

Begin with small, easy prompts like "What made me smile today?"

Stick

Be consistent, even if you only write for a few minutes.

Share

Join a journaling group or share your reflections with a trusted friend for encouragement.

Personal vignette

I once had a project with a short deadline, but I was preoccupied and couldn't devote enough time to it, making me anxious. I began to write down my thoughts on a piece of paper. I wrote for a few minutes, and my anxiety began to reduce. But I found that it reduced even more after twelve hours. I journaled again the next day, and for ten more days after that. It benefitted me hugely. Not only was I more relaxed and happier; I was also more focused on my project.

A brief activity to cultivate journaling

Think of something you are currently struggling with. It might be a stressful situation, an ambitious goal, a negative habit or a personal challenge. Write it down in your journal. Use it as a prompt. Now, using this prompt, start writing. Keep going for three minutes. Write whatever comes to your mind. Don't judge anything. If no thoughts come, you can simply write that no thought is coming, or you can just keep moving the pen or pencil. Once you've finished writing, read what you've written once or twice and see what insights you can find. Think how you might like to use those insights. You can use the same prompt for a few days. You can assess the impact of journaling on your emotional states, stress and happiness, and you can share its positive benefits with trustworthy people in your network.

Reflective questions

1. What are the key issues in your current personal and professional life for which you would like to use journaling?
2. How does writing help you become a better observer of your own life?
3. What are some important prompts that may help you start journaling?
4. With whom can you form journaling groups for mutual encouragement and learning?
5. What times in the day are most convenient for you to journal?
6. How will you assess the impact of journaling on you?
7. What did you learn from Sam's story?

References and further reading

Argudo, J. (2021) Expressive writing to relieve academic stress at university level. *Profile Issues in Teachers Professional Development*, 23(2), 17-33.

Baikie, K. A., & Wilhelm, K. (2005) Emotional and physical health benefits of expressive writing. *Advances in Psychiatric Treatment*, 11(5), 338-346.

Bandura, A. (1997) *Self-efficacy: The exercise of control.* New York: W. H: Freeman

Cattelino, E., Testa, S., Calandri, E., Fedi, A., Gattino, S., Graziano, F., ... & Begotti, T. (2023) Self-efficacy, subjective well-being and positive coping in adolescents with regard to Covid-19 lockdown. *Current Psychology*, 42(20), 17304-17315.

Center for the Advancement of Well-Being. (n.d.). *Thriving together series: The mental health benefits of journaling.* George Mason University. Available at: https://wellbeing.gmu.edu/thriving-together-series-the-mental-health-benefits-of-journaling/ (accessed May 2025).

Clear, J. (2018) *Atomic Habits: An easy & proven way to build good habits & break bad ones.* Avery: New York, NY.

Crawford, A., Sellman, E., & Joseph, S. (2021) Journaling: A more mindful approach to researching a mindfulness-based intervention in a junior school. *International Journal of Qualitative Methods*, 20, 16094069211014771.

MacIsaac, A., Mushquash, A. R., & Wekerle, C. (2023) Writing yourself well: dispositional self-reflection moderates the effect of a smartphone app-based journaling intervention on psychological wellbeing across time. *Behaviour Change*, 40(4), 297-313.

Ramadhanti, D. (2024) The Role of Reflective Journaling in Creative Writing Learning. *Journal of Social and Scientific Education*, 16-22.

Richelle, J., & Alea, N. (2024) Stay positive: The effects of positive affect journaling on emotion when remembering COVID-19. *Journal of Creativity in Mental Health*, 19(4), 529-541.

Riddell, T., Nassif, J., Hategan, A., & Jarecki, J. (2020) Healthy habits: Positive psychology, journaling, meditation, and nature therapy. *Humanism and Resilience in Residency Training: A Guide to Physician Wellness*, 439-472.

Sheldon, K. M., & Lyubomirsky, S. (2006) How to increase and sustain positive emotion: The effects of expressing gratitude and visualizing best possible selves. *The Journal of Positive Psychology*, 1(2), 73-82.

Stevens, D. D., & Cooper, J. E. (2023) *Journal Keeping: How to use reflective writing for learning, teaching, professional insight and positive change.* Taylor & Francis.

Sudirman, A., Gemilang, A. V., & Kristanto, T. M. A. (2021) The power of reflective journal writing for university students from the EFL perspective. *Studies in English Language and Education*, 8(3), 1061-1079.

Waddington, J. (2023) Self-efficacy. *ELT Journal*, 77(2), 237-240.

K

Chapter 11:

Knowing

"There is only one cause of unhappiness: the false beliefs you have in your head, beliefs so widespread, so commonly held, that it never occurs to you to question them."

Anthony de Mello

In India, people often share an old folk tale about two friends strolling near a river at dusk. One of the friends saw something black floating in the river. He thought it was a blanket and jumped into the river to collect it. As he approached it, he began to cry out and struggled to stay afloat. The friend on the riverbank shouted to leave the blanket and come back. But the friend in the river replied that he wanted to leave the blanket, but the blanket was not leaving him. In fact, it was a crocodile, and it ate the friend who went into the river to collect it.

In real life, we sometimes get stuck in our thoughts and beliefs. We can open the way to a better and happier life if the grip of those beliefs is loosened. By thinking again and finding new perspectives, we can reduce the power of negative thoughts and beliefs. Knowing is putting effort into learning more about oneself and others, rather than sticking to old assumptions and preconceived ideas. Knowing involves reviewing our beliefs and thoughts about ourselves, others and situations. Researchers have found that our behaviour is driven by many biases. Some of these are related to self, and others relate to interpreting other people's behaviour.

In his book *Thinking, Fast and Slow*, Daniel Kahneman proposes that the human mind operates through two systems – System 1 and System 2.[46] System 1 is fast, automatic and requires minimal effort. It mainly operates on assumptions and biases. System 2 is slower, more deliberate and requires more effort. When we are trying to know something, we make a conscious effort, questioning our assumptions, and we use System 2. According to Kahneman, allowing the mind to rely too much on System 1 can impact our personal happiness. By using System 2, we can take a sustainable approach to living a happy and fulfilling life.

Knowing our own assumptions and biases may help us to be happier. When we make judgements about other people, we rarely have access to extensive information telling us whether they are competent, intelligent, trustworthy or socially desirable. Instead, we rely on heuristics such as stereotypes to make efficient decisions about how to behave towards them. We form impressions quickly, and these impressions are very resistant to reconsideration and change. And we often inflate the value of the information at our disposal, over-relying on this at the expense of attending to personal and situational variability. Premature ideas about a person's personality and behaviour fuel our natural tendency to 'tune out'.

---

46   Kahneman, 2011

Although searching for new and potentially useful information about people and situations that we encounter for the first time can be time- and energy-consuming, it prevents misjudgements and increases engagement, creativity and the type of mindful, compassionate style of communication that is attractive and desirable to other people. Searching for new and potentially useful information may lead to better relationships and satisfaction.

Our habitual thoughts, feelings, behaviours and goals are easily activated, pulling us toward common and well-worn assumptions as opposed to being sensitive to the unique hedonic or utilitarian value of acting differently. We commonly fail to detect new distinctions and opportunities in the immediate environment, and this can erode our psychological flexibility. Our prior knowledge interferes with our ability to appreciate the unique, novel distinctions of new situations. We are relatively insensitive to context and perspective in the present when there is the potential to rely on prior knowledge and experience.

According to Stefan Klein, author of the book *The Science of Happiness*, 'the brain is the central switchboard for good feelings.[47] Unfortunately, it has a tendency to twist and turn in ways that sometimes prevent us from being as happy as we could be. We accept these sleights-of-mind not because they are useful, but because we are not aware of them.' He further stressed that, 'We all have illusions about what's good for us. But it's easy to avoid these mistakes and become more aware of what makes us happy and unhappy. What's important is to have a good perspective and to choose the right moment.'

47   Klein, 2006

In our hectic lives, it is easy to believe that satisfaction comes from achievement, keeping busy and striving for excellence. This touching story from Ioanna Iordanou tells otherwise:

I have always wondered: what exactly is happiness? Is it an intense feeling of joy, satisfaction or even elation? Or is it a quieter state – inner peace and contentment, even in the face of life's daily challenges? Whatever it may be, I thought I had lost touch with it. With a small toddler, a full-time job and a global pandemic, I felt like I was merely surviving. My days were a constant balancing act, striving to excel at work while being fully present for my little one.

The hardest part of the day was always the evenings – what parents around the world call 'bedtime'. After waking at the crack of dawn to cram everything into an overstimulating day, I dreaded those two hours of protest before my child finally surrendered to sleep. Despite a full day of daycare play and endless activities at home, she was never tired. And she wouldn't sleep without me by her side. Every night, I had to sit with her in the dark, holding her tiny hand as one minute stretched into ten, then into an hour. It felt torturous. I was exhausted, frustrated, angry – I just wanted to crawl into my own bed and have a moment of peace.

But one day, I decided to let go of the frustration and embrace the moment. I accepted it, and in doing so, I saw the gift hidden within. That hour of stillness, silence and simply being was a rare treasure. My child needed me – just my presence, my hand in hers as she drifted to sleep. And in that gift of quiet time, I found something unexpected: a sense of calm, gratitude and profound contentment.

It was happiness.

Ioanna's story reminds us that happiness can emerge in the stillness, even during life's most challenging times. By letting go of her frustration at time 'wasted' while her daughter drifted off to sleep, Ioanna came to know that it is often in the quietest moments – in this case, precious time spent with a sleepy child – that true happiness can be found.

Knowing and happiness

Delaying our judgements and searching for more information about ourselves and others can give us new perspectives. Applying psychological flexibility in the form of collecting additional information and not inflating the value of the information available to us may contribute to our health and happiness. According to Adam Grant, '… if you master the art of rethinking, I believe you will be better positioned for success at work and happiness in life'.[48] He continues, 'Thinking again can help you generate new solutions to old problems and revisit old solutions to new problems. It's a path to learning from the people around you and living with fewer regrets.'

When we question assumptions, we break free from our former selves. This liberates us and leads to more fulfilment. In their book *Happy for No Reason,* Marci Shimoff and Carol Kline suggest that 'Your thoughts don't always give you an accurate picture of reality, yet your mind goes on broadcasting them anyway. When you shine a light on your negative thoughts – and see that you don't have to believe them – it takes away much of their power to create misery.'[49] Putting extra effort in to know or question our own assumptions may give us more clarity about our worries or the challenges we are facing. This may reduce stress and anxiety and enhance positive emotions. As our aspirations and choices keep changing, questioning them and knowing what matters most may lead to greater fulfilment, satisfaction and happiness.

Knowing more about our own aspirations will help us to decide where we would like to spend our time and attention. By doing so, we will live a more meaningful life leading to happiness and overall well-being. Reassessing our beliefs about what happiness is and what constitutes it may inspire us to shift our energies and shift our focus towards its real sources. Similarly, rethinking the reasons for other people's behaviour may loosen the grip of negativity and enhance our relationship with them. Knowing the intentions behind their behaviour may help us to understand them and their context appropriately, leading to calmness and a relaxed mind.

---

48   Grant, 2023
49   Shimoff & Klein, 2009

In my Science of Happiness class, I ask students to make a list of acts that contribute to pleasure and happiness for them. Then, I ask them to make a second list of acts they engage in which contribute towards meaning, self-expression, using potential and growth. I then ask them to compare the two lists and share what they have learned. Most say that the activity gives them an understanding of what contributes to pleasure and what contributes to authenticity, and that this rethinking helps them to understand what they can do to find sustainable happiness.

Scientific evidence

Exploratory and novelty-seeking tendencies lead us to focus on activities that facilitate learning, competence and self-determination from which enduring meaning and well-being can be derived. In a study assessing adults with obesity, it was found that psychological flexibility significantly affected psychological well-being. In his book *Think Again*, Adam Grant shares an example of a time he made a presentation at a conference at which Nobel prize winner Daniel Kahneman was also in attendance. Adam says that Daniel enjoyed realizing that he had been wrong in his previous thinking about the concept of give and take and success, and that he felt happy because he knew that his ideas were now more accurate.[50]

Being surprised by the new things we might discover by rethinking our ideas and beliefs may boost our positive emotions. Thus, it may be argued that finding we are wrong about something is not a blow; it is a gift. So, ask yourself: when was the last time you enjoyed being wrong?!

Cultivating knowing

To cultivate the habit of knowing and rethinking, it's important to acknowledge that the human mind has biases and assumptions. An occasional review of our own assumptions about our behavioural patterns and other people's behaviour may be helpful. Reading about common biases can help increase our understanding of our own. In his book *Think Again*, Adam Grant shares that the simplest way to start rethinking our options is to question what we do daily.

---

50   Grant, 2023

Thinking like a scientist can help us to develop the habit of knowing or thinking again. It is always better to collect data before forming opinions, and to remain open to changing those opinions in the light of new data. Normally, our biases lead us to collect or interpret information in ways that strengthen views we already hold. To develop the habit of knowing and rethinking, we need to seek out information that goes against our views. When we find that we have made a mistake and discover something new, we should not be afraid to laugh at ourselves. Embracing the joy of being wrong can help us to develop the habit of knowing more and thinking again.

To assist us, we can request friends and family members to challenge our opinions in healthy ways. We all need people to act as thoughtful critics. Building a close group of such people to act as a sounding board can help us to develop the habit of rethinking and seeking to know more, and we can solicit their feedback on our plans, opinions, beliefs and execution strategies. Whenever you catch yourself thinking a negative thought, you can check to see whether it's the truth. This kind of occasional checking can help in building the habit of rethinking.

Personal vignette

I used to watch TV on my own a lot, and I thought this made me happy. However, a few years ago I realized that watching TV wasn't enhancing my happiness after all – at least not in proportion to the amount of time I was investing in it. Coming to this understanding helped me to refocus my time on things that really did enhance my happiness. Now I spend more time playing with my kids, teaching them and watching TV socially with family members.

A brief activity to cultivate knowing

Set some time aside to think about one assumption you have about your own behaviour. For example, it might be an assumption that scrolling through social media is quite relaxing. Check whether this is based on evidence or your own bias. Explore it by asking 'How do I feel before and after spending time on social media scrolling?' Consider whether questioning your assumption impacts your behaviour. Check if it makes you happier and calmer in your life. Similarly, write down an assumption you have about someone else's behaviour. For example, 'My family don't care about me'. Follow the same steps to review the assumption, then assess the impact of reviewing it and knowing more about your behaviour and emotional states.

Reflective questions

1. Which assumptions about your own behaviour may contribute to a happier and calmer mind if they were questioned?

2. How can you remind yourself to pause and question your own assumptions?

3. Are there any areas in your life where assumptions cause unnecessary stress and reduce your calmness and happiness?

4. How can you approach others with curiosity rather than judgement?

5. Are there instances where your assumptions about another person's behaviour turned out to be wrong? What did you learn from them?

6. How can you be more knowing rather than assuming in your interpretation of other people's behaviour?

7. How can you be more sceptical of your negative thoughts?

8. What did you learn from Ioanna's story?

References and further reading

Gilovich, T., Griffin, D., & Kahneman, D. (Eds) (2002) *Heuristics and Biases: The psychology of intuitive judgment*. Cambridge university press.

Grant, A. (2023) *Think Again: The power of knowing what you don't know*. Penguin.

Guerrini Usubini, A., Varallo, G., Granese, V., Cattivelli, R., Consoli, S., Bastoni, I., ... & Molinari, E. (2021) The impact of psychological flexibility on psychological well-being in adults with obesity. *Frontiers in Psychology*, 12, 636933.

Kahneman, D. (2011) *Thinking, Fast and Slow*. Farrar, Straus and Giroux.

Kammrath, L. K., Ames, D. R., & Scholer, A. A. (2007) Keeping up impressions: Inferential rules for impression change across the Big Five. *Journal of Experimental Social Psychology*, 43(3), 450-457.

Kashdan, T. (2009) *Curious? Discover the missing ingredient to a fulfilling life*. William Morrow & Co.

Kashdan, T. B., & Rottenberg, J. (2010) Psychological flexibility as a fundamental aspect of health. *Clinical Psychology Review*, 30(7), 865-878.

Kashdan, T. B., & Steger, M. F. (2007) Curiosity and pathways to well-being and meaning in life: Traits, states, and everyday behaviors. *Motivation and Emotion*, 31, 159-173.

Klein, S. (2006). *The Science of Happiness: How our brains make us happy – and what we can do to get happier*. Marlowe/Avalon Publishing Group.

Shimoff, M., & Kline, C. (2009) *Happy for No Reason: 7 steps to being happy from the inside out*. Simon and Schuster.

L

Chapter 12:

Learning

"Learning is the only thing the mind never exhausts, never fears, and never regrets."

Leonardo da Vinci

Every act of learning is a quiet conversation between the mind and the soul – where curiosity whispers and happiness blooms. Learning always contributes to happiness. Learning is a process of acquiring new knowledge, skills, attitude, thinking and behaviours. Learning can take either a formal or informal route. We learn many things and activities without undergoing any formal training. We learn by observing others, by reading, by having new experiences, by meeting people and going to new places, and through introspection.

We also undergo formal learning processes for many things, particularly education and training related to jobs and careers. We may take formal training for hobbies, special performances and social events too. Intentional learning generates positive emotions and leads to happiness; however, mandatory learning that we are compelled to engage in can also help us achieve our goals and, in the long run, enhance satisfaction and life fulfilment. Learning is an innate urge, and, through its satisfaction, it leads to happiness. Learning is not just about acquiring knowledge; it's about awakening new possibilities within ourselves.

Learning and happiness

Learning for personal development enhances our happiness. There are many examples of different forms of learning contributing to personal development – such as learning to walk, throw a ball, make a recipe, drive a car or operate a new app. Such opportunities for personal development through learning occur at all ages. Learning can also increase the choices available to us. This growth enhances our self-esteem and contributes to the satisfaction of our needs, leading to enhanced happiness and well-being.

Learning helps us to understand our problems and gives us new ideas to handle them, which reduces our stress and anxiety. By learning new skills, we can adapt to new circumstances and bounce back from adversity and trauma. Learning satisfies our curiosity and, by exploring and understanding, leads to joy and happiness. Learning activities that are interesting and challenging may generate flow experiences, leading to reductions in stress and increases in happiness. Learning may give immediate joy and long-term fulfilment.

In the midst of a busy life, it's easy to feel disconnected from joy. Jane Daly shares how, through a chance encounter, she found a new way to reconnect with her own happiness:

I often feel as though my life is running on autopilot. Between curating my dreams and juggling family responsibilities, I rarely have a moment to pause. Beneath my busy exterior, I often feel disconnected and unsure of how to rediscover joy.

One evening, I became engrossed in an online conversation about a new book, 'Regenerative Learning: Nurturing People and Caring for the Planet' by Satish Kumar. This promised more than just gardening skills – it offered a chance to reconnect with the Earth and myself. Although hesitant, my curiosity about regenerative learning, which emphasizes harmony between people and the planet, drew me in. Letting my attention ebb and flow, I learned about soil regeneration, biodiversity and sustainable living. But what surprised me most was how the process resonated with me emotionally. I discovered that learning isn't just a cognitive act – it's deeply innate and tied to my emotions, helping me uncover more about myself.

As I planted metaphorical seeds and observed growth, I began to reflect on my own needs and desires. For me, there is a profound connection between learning and happiness. Engaging in meaningful, exploratory learning activates the brain's reward system, releasing dopamine and fostering well-being. For me, each small success in my flourishing metaphorical garden brought me a sense of accomplishment, purpose and mindfulness.

My garden is now my sanctuary – a space where I find joy, confidence and self-discovery. By embracing learning as a regenerative and emotional process, I have not only nurtured the Earth but also cultivated a deeper understanding of myself and my capacity for happiness.

Jane's story illustrates the deep emotional connection between learning and personal fulfilment, revealing how exploring new knowledge can be a powerful path to self-discovery. Through this journey of learning and growth, Jane has discovered that, for her, nurturing both the Earth and herself can be the key to cultivating lasting happiness.

Scientific evidence

A life of curiosity-driven learning helps us to acquire skills in perspective-taking, empathy and creativity, which can contribute to better relationships and fulfilment. A love of learning can contribute to a good life, which goes beyond happiness. Learning may also satisfy our need for competence, which, as per self-determination theory discussed in Chapter 2, boosts well-being.

Learning strengthens our abilities and skills, which contributes to enhancing self-efficacy. This in turn contributes to increased happiness. Learning contributes to self-esteem, resilience, self-acceptance, hope and communication, all of which contribute to happiness. Table 12.1 explores how different learning types contribute to happiness.

Table 12.1: Types of learning and their contribution to happiness

Type of learning	Examples	Contribution to happiness
Personal development	Learning a new language, meditation, cooking	Boosts confidence, sense of growth
Professional development	Learning new software, leadership skills	Enhances self-efficacy, career satisfaction
Curiosity-based learning	Reading about a specific subject, such as history or science	Joy of discovery, mental stimulation
Experiential learning	Travelling, volunteering	Builds empathy, connection, resilience
Coping learning	Mindfulness, stress management	Reduces anxiety, increases well-being

Cultivating learning

Exploring the motivation behind your desire to learn is the most important step towards incorporating more of it into your life. Knowing why it matters and how it will impact you will encourage you to get involved in the learning process. You may also recognize the gut feelings you have for learning something new in terms of skills, attitude, thinking or behaviour, and acknowledging these feelings can inspire you to take the initiative in your learning.

Embracing challenges as opportunities may inspire you to engage in learning to help you handle those challenges and move forward in your life and career. Having a curious mindset may also nudge you to enrol in learning opportunities to satisfy your curiosity and enhance your understanding. Recognizing the need to change in order to adapt to new circumstances boosts motivation to learn and understand, and acknowledging current challenges and anticipating future ones will also inspire you to engage in learning. Setting higher goals for your career and life can also inspire you to engage in learning in order to achieve those goals.

Seek out projects and initiatives that require learning new knowledge and skills. These will nudge you to engage in new learning. Adopt a growth mindset and keep exploring new technologies and approaches which may be helpful in your career and your life in general. Observe people who are always keen to learn, and, if possible, talk to them to understand their motivations – their insights may inspire you to persist in what you are trying to achieve.

Setting learning goals can also be helpful in motivating you to keep investing time and energy in your endeavours. You can also add a fun element to the learning process so that you remain engaged even with difficult learning activities. Celebrating when you achieve your learning goals can help inspire you to learn more. Having group experiences or peer learning can also enhance your motivation to learn, as mutual discussion and motivating each other can help a group to stay together and invest their time and effort in learning.

The following flowchart can be used to cultivate learning:

Curiosity/challenge
↓
Set learning goals
↓
Engage in small steps daily
↓
Reflect and celebrate progress
↓
Apply learning
↓
Happiness and growth

Personal vignette

When I was learning a statistical data analysis tool during my PhD, I travelled for four hours to get help from an instructor. I did this for a few weeks; it was exhausting, but it helped me immensely and I gained great satisfaction from it. In a sense, this satisfaction is no different from our earliest learning; when my son was learning to walk, the happiness of the family whenever he took a few steps motivated him to keep going. He still loves to learn new things.

A brief activity to cultivate learning

Make a group of three or four members by inviting colleagues, friends or family. The objective of the group is to share and strengthen learning with each other. Encourage each member to teach everyone else at least one thing they don't know. Ask each member of the group to add an element of fun to the way they teach. After all the members have shared, ask each of them to reflect on their learning and how it has added to their happiness.

Reflective questions

1. How has learning contributed to your happiness and satisfaction?

2. When was the last time you felt fully engaged in learning something?

3. Which new activities might enhance your happiness by learning about them?

4. What do you need to learn to handle your current challenges and difficulties?

5. What knowledge, skills and attitudes may help you strengthen your relationships?

6. What one thing would you like to learn to do to the best of your ability in your career?

7. Write down a recent moment when you learned something new. How did it make you feel?

8. How might having learning goals contribute to enhancing your happiness?

9. What did you learn from Jane's story?

References and further reading

Chueh, D. A., Hen, C., & Lim, Y. X. (2023) Perceived stress, resilience, self-esteem as predictors of life satisfaction among university students in Malaysia (Doctoral dissertation, UTAR).

Csikszentmihalyi, M. (2013) *Flow: The psychology of happiness*. Random House.

Deci, E. L., & Ryan, R. M. (2012) Self-determination Theory. In: P. A. M. Van Lange, A. W. Kruglanski, & E. T. Higgins (Eds), *Handbook of Theories of Social Psychology* (pp. 416–436).

Maurer, T. J. (2001) Career-relevant learning and development, worker age, and beliefs about self-efficacy for development. *Journal of Management*, 27(2), 123-140.

Obhi, H. K., Hardy, A., & Margrett, J. A. (2021) Values of lifelong learners and their pursuits of happiness and whole-person wellness. *Aging & mental health*, 25(4), 672-678.

Oishi, S., & Westgate, E. C. (2022) A psychologically rich life: Beyond happiness and meaning. *Psychological Review*, 129(4), 790.

Siebert, A. (2009) *The Resiliency Advantage: Master change, thrive under pressure, and bounce back from setbacks*. ReadHowYouWant. com.

Suh, H., Kim, S., Hwang, S., & Han, S. (2020) Enhancing preservice teachers' key competencies for promoting sustainability in a University Statistics Course. *Sustainability*, 12(21), 9051.

Tooby, J., & Cosmides, L. (1990) The past explains the present: Emotional adaptations and the structure of ancestral environments. *Ethology and Sociobiology*, 11(4–5), 375–424.

M

Chapter 13:

Meaning

"Life is never made unbearable by circumstances,
but only by lack of meaning and purpose."

Viktor E. Frankl

Every act – whether large or small – is meaningful when it brings happiness to others. Every act holds the potential to become meaningful when we discover how it touches the lives of others. Meaning is a sense of connection to something greater than oneself – a sense of purpose in life. It is linked to life satisfaction and happiness. Meaning provides direction and deeper fulfilment. It is a facilitator of adaptive coping and a marker of therapeutic growth. Meaning provides motivation to pursue goals and activities despite difficulties and challenges.

Meaning and happiness

Meaning gives purpose and direction to our lives and encourages us to focus our energy and efforts on activities that resonate with our core values, leading to satisfaction and fulfilment. It acts as an anchor during stormy times, keeping us steady despite stress and challenges, and thus it helps us to maintain positive emotional states. Meaning helps us persist when there is little or no support available. It gives us the ability to persevere and keeps us on the right track, moving us forward towards our goals and contributing to our ongoing well-being.

A core element of meaning is focusing on others and engaging in meaningful activities that help enhance the social dimension of well-being. By focusing on the welfare of other people, we develop positive relationships with them, which contributes to enhanced happiness and satisfaction. Meaning provides us with an intrinsic motivation, and inspires us to give our best, even in the absence of any external recognition. Psychotherapists have begun to recommend engaging in social service to their clients who suffer from depression and other psychological problems, as it can lead to better psychological functioning for them. During existential crises, many people opt for meaningful work that helps them have fulfilling life experiences.

When we are engaged in meaningful activities with a focus on others and the overall betterment of our community or even society, we may receive formal recognition and appreciation, adding to our sense of satisfaction and encouraging us to do more. When we engage in purposeful things with wider meaning, there is a greater chance of our family and friends joining forces with us in those causes, which further enhances our fulfilment.

Neal Sundberg shares a heartfelt letter to his unborn son, Oliver, revealing how the anticipation of fatherhood reshaped his purpose and deepened his happiness:

Dear Oliver,

I am writing to you in hope that you find meaning in your life – your 'why' – just as I have found mine. Your mother is sixteen weeks pregnant today with you in her belly.

Throughout my life I have found this 'why' in all sorts of things. My career, being a good friend, helping others and so much more. Over the last six months, I left my 'perfect on paper' job, I haven't seen my friends as often as I would like, and I haven't given enough time to volunteering. Though a few days after we found out that mommy was pregnant, I was up early drinking my coffee alone and contemplating life. You'll realize this when you get older – your dad is in his head a lot, and your mom likes to sleep in.

Anyways, I was thinking about becoming a father and I had the most calming feeling sweep over me. I didn't feel overwhelmed. I felt still. It was the calmest I have felt in a long time. I soon realized this stillness came because in that moment, life felt simple. It was as if things made sense and my 'why' became clear – the responsibility I have to you.

While I know you are going to be the most amazing and well-behaved baby ever, I also know that raising a child is incredibly difficult. Friedrich Nietzsche once said, 'He who has a why to live can bear almost any how.' When you are an angsty teenager, I might let you read his books. Until then, what he meant was that when life is difficult, knowing your 'why' or the meaning you give to what you are doing can get you through any challenge.

Even when I am fighting off urine while changing your diaper, I will reflect on my why – the responsibility I have to be the best father that I can be for you. As I get you all cleaned up and change into a new shirt myself, I have no doubt that happiness will be present.

> *So, my dear Oliver, my hope for you is that you stay curious, kind and resilient as you navigate the world. Life won't always be simple, and you'll face challenges just as I have. But remember, happiness isn't found when everything is perfect. It comes from knowing that you are living your life with purpose – taking steps that align with your values and the meaning you have crafted along the way.*
>
> *And no matter what, know that I will always be here, walking beside you, cheering you on, and loving you unconditionally. Because, my dear Oliver, as of today, that is my why.*
>
> *Love,*
> *Dad*

This heartfelt reflection reminds us that the pursuit of meaning in life – whether through personal responsibilities or larger goals – can bring clarity, purpose and a deep sense of happiness. Finding out 'why' brings clarity and resilience against life's challenges. And, just as Neal found his 'why' in becoming a father, we too can uncover meaning in our daily lives, guiding us through challenges and bringing us fulfilment along the way.

Scientific evidence

There is plenty of empirical evidence that finding and maintaining meaning in one's life affects well-being, acts as a bulwark against stressful situations, and is associated with positive outcomes. A meta-analysis of one hundred and forty-seven studies concluded that the experience of greater life meaning is robustly associated with higher subjective well-being.[51] The findings suggest that helping clients to experience meaning in their lives is important to helping them thrive.

In a study exploring the association between coronavirus stress, meaning in life, psychological flexibility and subjective well-being, researchers found that meaning in life mediated the effect of coronavirus stress on students' well-being.[52] In another study, researchers found that

---

51   Li, Dou & Liang, 2021
52   Arslan & Allen, 2022

experiencing meaning on an everyday basis is a desirable feature of a healthy and satisfactory life. They found that meaningfulness was more strongly associated with positive well-being.[53]

In a recent three-wave longitudinal study, the researchers found that having a sense of meaning in life predicted flourishing across several key measurements of well-being.[54] Meaning was also found to be related to positive and negative aspects of well-being through optimism.

The following flowchart illustrates how meaning unfolds in our lives:

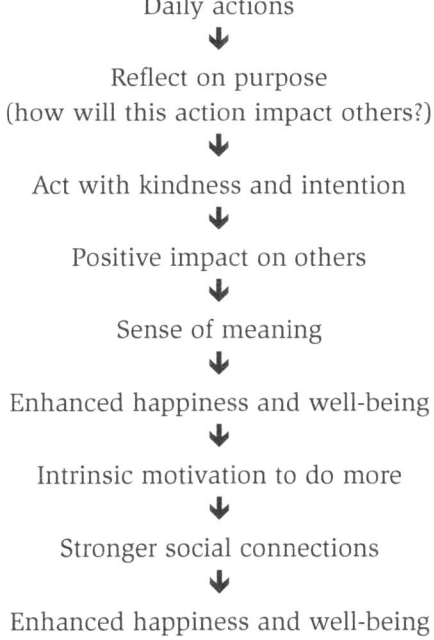

Daily actions
⬇
Reflect on purpose
(how will this action impact others?)
⬇
Act with kindness and intention
⬇
Positive impact on others
⬇
Sense of meaning
⬇
Enhanced happiness and well-being
⬇
Intrinsic motivation to do more
⬇
Stronger social connections
⬇
Enhanced happiness and well-being

Cultivating meaning

In the modern world, with all its distractions, work pressures and demands on one's time and attention, doing one's work with honesty can be seen as meaningful. We can make our lives meaningful by understanding our core values. We can seek volunteering opportunities

---

53   Crego *et al.*, 2020
54   Rudaz, Fincham & Ledermann, 2024

that resonate with our values. By observing other people who are engaged in purposeful work, we can gain inspiration and ideas about getting involved in purposeful work ourselves.

By recalling what we have achieved in our lives thanks to other people's support, we can find inspiration to support others in their lives and careers. Reading spiritual and religious texts may also motivate us to engage in purposeful work to help others. Identifying small acts that will bring smiles to others' faces can also increase meaning in life. Recalling happiness on the faces of people because of our good work may also encourage us to continue with that work.

Exploring the purpose of life and the actions we should engage in during our time on this planet may also inspire us to embrace a meaningful life. While exploring the purpose of life, we may seek help from a coach and a wise friend or family member. By exploring the contribution of nature towards humanity – the fresh air, clean water, flowers, fruits, grains and so many other things nature gives us – we can explore what we can do to contribute to making this planet a better place to live. Focusing on these contributions may inspire us to do something meaningful for others without expecting anything in return.

The following flowchart can be used to cultivate meaning in daily life:

Understand core values
↓
Identify small acts of kindness
↓
Engage in purposeful activities
↓
Reflect on how your actions help others
↓
Repeat consistently
↓
Enhanced meaning and happiness

Personal vignette

When doing things for others I always gain a sense of confidence, and I find that seeking help from others for purposeful tasks is very easy. I have also received a great deal of help while doing meaningful work for other people or communities. On a more personal level, I find teaching my seven-year-old son immensely satisfying. We learn and at the same time play together. While teaching him, I feel I am doing the most important thing in my life.

A brief activity to cultivate meaning

Invite family and friends for an informal discussion about meaning and happiness. Encourage each of them to share a recent experience that felt deeply meaningful to them. Ask them to share how that experience was meaningful to them and how it affected their happiness. Encourage everyone to speak and contribute something valuable to the discussion. Invite everyone to share what they have learned from the discussion and encourage them to explore how they can use those lessons in the future to enhance meaning in their lives.

Reflective questions

1. What can you do for others that gives you immense satisfaction?
2. What are the five most meaningful things in your life?
3. Think of five people who you think are contributing to other people's lives. What can you learn from them in relation to living a purposeful life?
4. How can you add more meaning to each day without using additional time or effort?
5. How has engaging in purposeful activities in the past affected your state of mind?
6. Have traumatic or extremely challenging events affected your life positively?
7. Might self-control help in having more meaning in your life?
8. What did you learn from Neal's story?

References and further reading

Arslan, G., & Allen, K. A. (2022) Exploring the association between coronavirus stress, meaning in life, psychological flexibility, and subjective well-being. *Psychology, Health & Medicine*, 27(4), 803-814.

Arslan, G., & Yıldırım, M. (2021) Coronavirus stress, meaningful living, optimism, and depressive symptoms: A study of moderated mediation model. *Australian Journal of Psychology*, 73(2), 113-124.

Aruta, J. J. B. R., Salanga, M. G. C., Pakingan, K. A., & Mateo, N. J. (2022) Blessed are the poor, they shall be more persistent: Meaning in life and persistence among adolescents from low-and high-income regions in the Philippines. *Psychological Studies*, 67(3), 294-303.

Crego, A., Yela, J. R., Gómez-Martínez, M. Á., & Karim, A. A. (2020) The contribution of meaningfulness and mindfulness to psychological well-being and mental health: A structural equation model. *Journal of Happiness Studies*, 21(8), 2827-2850.

Ho, M. Y., Cheung, F. M., & Cheung, S. F. (2010) The role of meaning in life and optimism in promoting well-being. *Personality and Individual Differences*, 48(5), 658-663.

Li, J. B., Dou, K., & Liang, Y. (2021) The relationship between presence of meaning, search for meaning, and subjective well-being: A three-level meta-analysis based on the meaning in life questionnaire. *Journal of Happiness Studies*, 22, 467-489.

McKnight, P. E., & Kashdan, T. B. (2009) Purpose in life as a system that creates and sustains health and well-being: An integrative, testable theory. *Review of General Psychology*, 13(3), 242-251.

Qiu, S. (2024) Exploration of the Relationship Between Goal Engagement Capability, Meaning in Life, and Well-being among College Students. *Journal of Modern Education and Culture*, 1(3).

Rudaz, M., Fincham, F. D., & Ledermann, T. (2024) Presence of meaning in life mediates the effects of gratitude and caring for bliss on flourishing in college students: A three-wave longitudinal study. *The Journal of Positive Psychology*, 19(6), 1011-1022.

Russo-Netzer, P., & Ameli, M. (2021) Optimal sense-making and resilience in times of pandemic: Integrating rationality and meaning in psychotherapy. *Frontiers in Psychology*, 12, 645926.

Sica, L. S., Parola, A., De Rosa, B., Sommantico, M., Fenizia, E., Postiglione, J., ... & Parrello, S. (2024) Meaning matters: a person-centered investigation of meaning in life, future time perspective, and well-being in young adults. *Journal for Person-Oriented Research*, 10(2), 104.

Steger, M. F., Frazier, P., Oishi, S., & Kaler, M. (2006) The meaning in life questionnaire: assessing the presence of and search for meaning in life. *Journal of Counseling Psychology*, 53(1), 80-93.

N

Chapter 14:

Nature

"In every walk with nature, one receives far more than he seeks."

John Muir

Nature holds the power to heal, inspire and awaken a deep sense of belonging within us. It is the physical world that envelops us, and it consists of all things living and non-living that are independent of human invention. It includes all the plants, animals, mountains, rivers, oceans, forests and skies, and the intricate ecosystems connecting them. The essence of life is embodied in nature – a magnificent yet modest, self-sustaining cycle of growth, decay and renewal.

More profoundly, nature serves as a reflection of our position in the cosmos, and a reminder of both our interconnectedness with all other living things and the limits of our power. More than just a background for our lives, it is a profound teacher that imparts wisdom, harmony, patience and growth. When we establish a connection with nature, we find paths to inner peace, contentment and a sense of purpose, in addition to the beauty of the world around us.

> **Nature can offer us a healing refuge. This story from Jolanta Burke tells of a young woman, overwhelmed by emotional turmoil, finding peace and hope in the calm of a forest:**
>
> *It was her against the world. Her adolescent shoulders ached from carrying the weight of it all – her mother in a hospital, her father tearing into her for all she held dear, and the distant memory of the last time she laughed that deep, satisfying belly laugh. As she stepped into the forest, the sound of twigs snapping beneath her feet jolted her back to the better times – carefree childhood, togetherness and joy.*
>
> *She gazed upon the tree canopies stretching above her and felt instant warmth in her heart and the joy of the gentle dance between the sun and the trees vying for her attention. As the sunlight touched her face, the branches stirred happily in response, protecting her in the shade. Soon, she joined their dance, lifting her eyes to the sky and swaying her hips with nature. She felt calm, grounded, and protected – she felt at one with nature and closed her eyes.*
>
> *A new side to the forest had opened up her senses, as she could hear the birds singing a symphony filled with different pitches at varied frequencies and a range of notes she had never noticed before. They were supported by the lazy buzz of friendly flies circling her joyfully. Then she heard dried up branches falling to the ground – or was it a squirrel foraging for food? She became aware of the restorative sound of the leaves rustling all around, making her eyes heavy and her muscles relaxed. She had to sit down.*

As she opened her eyes in search of a place to rest, she noticed a fallen tree a few steps away. She walked towards it mindfully, focused on the movement of each muscle in response to the uneven surface of the forest bed. She touched the bark with her fingers and pulled herself up on top of it while turning her head around, taking in everything her eyes could see.

She took a deep breath and closed her eyes again. She was hit with a myriad of aromas. The smell of damp moss, moist leaves, wet tree trunks, rocks, pine needles and unidentified forest fragrances teased her nostrils as she began to slow down her breathing. She checked her emotions, and, to her surprise, she was now filled with hope, calm, and a deep connection to the buzzing flies, the drumming woodpeckers and the warm forest embracing her lovingly.

She opened her eyes and looked around her again. Five minutes ago, she felt lonely, scared, and angry. Now, nature's embrace made her heart jump, her emotions soar and her dreams emerge. It transformed her unbearable life into the place of safety and belonging.

She was in her happy place again.

In nature's embrace, Jolanta rediscovered what was lost – peace, joy, serenity and a sense of belonging. Her story serves as a reminder that nature has the power to heal and restore us, helping to reconnect us to the simple joys of life and, ultimately, to our own happiness.

Nature and happiness

Experiences of nature's grandeur evoke awe, inspiring gratitude and a sense of connection – essential ingredients for happiness. Time spent in nature gives us clarity, serves as an outlet for the chaos going on in our mind and provides new perspectives on situations. Stepping into nature fosters a sense of connection with the outdoor world. Sometimes, a warm sunny day gives us all the comfort we need to keep going. Being surrounded by trees, flowers, animals, clouds, a clear day or night sky and even people, builds a sense of awe and a bond with something larger than ourselves. Time spent in nature helps us ground ourselves and better understand life. It brings out the best in us – and this leads to joy and peace.

Spending time in nature also enhances acceptance towards life situations, helping us to better navigate the various issues and challenges we face, supporting peace of mind and overall life satisfaction. Greenery, fresh air and sunlight improve our physical and psychological health. The beautiful sights and smells of nature, like the petals and fragrances of flowers, makes us happy. It helps us to appreciate life's simple joys and to experience a deeper sense of well-being. All traditions of the world recognize the healing powers of nature. In their book *Ikigai*, Héctor García and Francesc Miralles recommend that we should return to nature often to recharge our batteries.[55] Returning to nature will enhance our happiness and longevity.

Scientific evidence

Contact with nature is increasingly recognized as enhancing human health and well-being. There are a number of scientific studies that highlight the importance of nature and explore how it can affect our happiness. A study conducted by Capaldi *et al* with eight and half thousand participants found a significant positive relationship between connection to nature and happiness. They found that individuals who felt more connected to nature tended to have or experience higher levels of positive emotions and life satisfaction.[56] In another study conducted in Finland, researchers found that most of the participants agreed that nature makes them happy.[57] Richard Louv introduced the concept of 'nature-deficit disorder' in his book *Last Child in the Woods*. He argues that regular exposure to natural environments can improve attention, reduce stress, and boost mood.[58]

George MacKerron and Susana Mourato conducted a unique study to explore the relationship between individuals' immediate environments

---

55   García & Miralles, 2017
56   Capaldi, Dopko & Zelenski, 2014
57   Hakoköngäs & Puhakka, 2023
58   Louv, 2008

and momentary subjective well-being.[59] They developed a smartphone app and used it to collect over one million responses from more than twenty thousand participants at random moments while using GPS satellite positioning to determine their geographic coordinates. They found that participants were significantly and substantially happier outdoors in natural habitats than they were in urban environments. Connection to nature is deeply rooted in evolutionary psychology, and human brains and bodies respond positively to natural settings, all of which leads to a relaxed body and mind.

Cultivating nature

To cultivate a connection to nature, start incorporating it into your daily and weekly routine. This might be small rituals, such as watching the sunrise or sunset, meditating outdoors or gardening. You might also engage in birdwatching, stargazing or observing plants and trees. If you don't have a garden, you could spend time observing flowers on your balcony or in a nearby park. Take mindful nature walks. Reducing screen time, and fill that freed-up time with outdoor activities may enhance your sense of connection to nature. Adding potted plants to your balcony garden or rooftop can enhance the time spent with nature to some extent.

You could partner with a nature-loving friend, who will help motivate you to spend more time in nature, and then stick to a regular schedule for your outdoor activities together. Being in nature with someone else can heighten the joy of the experience. You might also join nature clubs or groups. These provide opportunities for active engagement and enhance the overall commitment to nature, leading to enhanced happiness and satisfaction in life.

59   McKerron & Mourato, 2013

Personal vignette

Sometimes, when my stress or anxiety reaches a peak, it really helps just to take a walk around nature. As someone who grew up with nature, I know how it feels to step on cool, soft grass on a summer evening, or what the breeze after a garden gets watered feels like. And I know what it does to your mind – it's truly amazing. It's said that walking barefoot on grass even helps your body's circulatory system. You just can't stop it from making you happier.

A brief activity for cultivating nature

When it comes to nature, small actions can create powerful ripples of happiness. Try these simple practices to nurture your bond with nature – one moment at a time:

1. **Nature pause:** Spend five minutes observing the sky, trees or flowers around you – notice the colours, sounds and scents.

2. **Mindful nature walk:** Walk slowly in a nearby park or garden. Tune in to the sounds of birds, the rustling leaves, or the feel of sunlight on your skin.

3. **Gratitude for nature:** Each day, appreciate one thing in nature – a blooming flower, a fresh breeze, or the warmth of sunlight.

4. **Nature journaling:** Capture your nature experiences with a few lines or sketches each day – what you saw, felt or discovered.

5. **Green companion:** Care for a small plant at home – water it mindfully and observe its slow but steady growth.

Reflective questions

1. Recall some of your previous experiences of time spent in nature. Which experience brought you the most happiness?

2. How can you spend more time with nature to boost your happiness in everyday life?

3. What can you do to involve your family and friends in nature connection activities?

4. What did you learn from Jolanta's story?

References and further reading

Bethelmy, L. C., & Corraliza, J. A. (2019) Transcendence and sublime experience in nature: Awe and inspiring energy. *Frontiers in Psychology*, 10, 509.

Capaldi, C. A., Dopko, R. L., & Zelenski, J. M. (2014) The relationship between nature connectedness and happiness: A meta-analysis. *Frontiers in Psychology*, 5, 92737.

DeVille, N. V., Tomasso, L. P., Stoddard, O. P., Wilt, G. E., Horton, T. H., Wolf, K. L., Brymer, E., Kahn, P.H., & James, P. (2021) Time spent in nature is associated with increased pro-environmental attitudes and behaviors. *International Journal of Environmental Research and Public Health*, 18(14), 7498.

García, H., & Miralles, F. (2017) *Ikigai: The Japanese secret to a long and happy life*. Penguin.

Hakoköngäs, E., & Puhakka, R. (2023) Happiness from nature? Adolescents' conceptions of the relation between happiness and nature in Finland. *Leisure Sciences*, 45(7), 665-683.

Kellert, S. R. (2012) *Building for Life: Designing and understanding the human-nature connection*. Island press.

Lewis, C. A. (1996) *Green Nature/Human Nature: The meaning of plants in our lives*. University of Illinois press.

Louv, R. (2008) *Last Child in the Woods: Saving our children from nature-deficit disorder*. Algonquin books.

MacKerron, G., & Mourato, S. (2013) Happiness is greater in natural environments. *Global Environmental Change*, 23(5), 992-1000.

Richardson, M., Passmore, H. A., Lumber, R., Thomas, R., & Hunt, A. (2021) Moments, not minutes: The nature-wellbeing relationship. *International Journal of Wellbeing*, 11(1), 8–33.

Schroeder, H. W. (2021) *Ecology of the Heart: Understanding how people experience natural environments*. In: A. W. Ewert (Ed), *Natural Resource Management: The human dimension* (pp13–27). Routledge.

West, R., & Pelser, A. C. (2015) Perceiving God through natural beauty. *Faith and Philosophy*, 32(3), 293–312.

O

Chapter 15:

Optimism

"Optimism is a happiness magnet.
If you stay positive, good things and good
people will be drawn to you."

Mary Lou Retton

When life brings challenges, why do some people see walls while others see doors waiting to be opened? Or, to put it another way, why do some people smile through struggles while others sink under stress? The secret often lies in their mindset, a positive belief that good things are possible, even when life feels uncertain. This ability to see a light at the end of the tunnel is called optimism – the invisible force that keeps us going, even when the road is tough.

Psychologists Michael Scheier and Charles Carver describe optimism as the stable tendency 'to believe that good rather than bad things will happen'.[60] Optimism is a global expectation that the future will bring a bounty of good things and a scarcity of bad things. According to their self-regulation model, expectations and confidence are important when individuals face challenges and obstacles to goal achievement. When optimistic people face difficulties, they believe that they can overcome them and therefore they persist in their efforts. Optimistic people explain bad things in such a manner as 'to account for the role of other people and environments in producing bad outcomes (i.e., an external attribution), to interpret the bad events as not likely to happen again (i.e., a variable attribution), and to constrain the bad outcome to just one performance area and not others (i.e., a specific attribution).'

An optimistic attitude pays significant dividends in health and happiness. Many studies have found that optimists enjoy better mental and physical health. Optimism is regarded as the best personal resource for fostering resistance to distress. It is positively associated with self-mastery, self-esteem, well-being, performance and social relationships, and it is negatively associated with neuroticism, anxiety and depression. Martin Seligman conceptualized optimism as an explanatory style, and described it as people's characteristic way of explaining events.[61]

This story from Gina Phelps Thoebes shares how Marcus, a physician leader, was able to transform his critical inner voice into a more supportive and optimistic one:

"My mind is bombarded with thoughts about how I'm about to fail – it paralyzes me and keeps me stuck," Marcus confessed to his coach.

"It sounds like a critical voice in your head is holding you hostage," his coach reflected back.

---

60   Scheier & Carver, 1985
61   Seligman, 1998

"Yes! Sometimes I feel like a hostage of my own mind, despite all my success."

Marcus's coach asked that they explore this critical voice further together. Marcus identified that the voice reminded him of both a critical parent and a critical boss he had in the past. After working through Marcus' experience, his coach asked him to identify other perspectives.

"Who have been your biggest champions in life? What would they say if they had the microphone, instead of the critical voice holding it?"

Marcus named his wife and his mentor, who had both been vocal about their belief in him. He committed to experiment with passing his internal microphone around between sessions – first to name the critical voice when it reared its head, and then to deliberately pass the microphone to one of his champions and allow them to share an optimistic perspective.

At their next session, Marcus shared how things were going. He admitted he felt a bit silly, naming the voices, but at the same time said he felt lighter every time he did.

"Optimism is contagious. When they say I can be wildly successful, a little bit of that same belief grows inside of me."

It truly was contagious, as the small intentional shifts to optimistic thinking started to have a ripple effect throughout his personal and professional life. Marcus shared what he was doing with his wife, who was proud to know she was one of his champion voices and would prompt him with "who is holding the microphone?" when she saw him starting to worry.

Optimism even startled trickling into how Marcus led. He strived intentionally to be one of the champion voices for those in his charge. He knew he was making an impact when several of his direct reports credited him as a driving force in their ability to achieve their potential.

The critical voice still grabs the microphone occasionally, but now Marcus's optimistic voices get a lot more airtime, which has led to him feeling more joy and confidence in his daily life.

Gina's account is a good example of how a shift in perspective can not only empower us to embrace our potential, but also spread optimism to those around us, fostering happiness and reinforcing the profound impact of a positive mindset on both personal and professional growth.

Optimism and happiness

Optimists have higher levels of motivation and perseverance than people who are less optimistic. Due to this, optimists are more likely to achieve more of their goals, leading to increased happiness. Optimism is also associated with reduced stress and anxiety. Optimists cope better with difficult situations, leading to higher well-being. When we have high levels of optimism, we tend to have a positive outlook on life and this leads to raised levels excitement and anticipation, generating happiness. Optimism also positively impacts our relationships with other people, and these better relationships also contribute to our happiness.

Scientific evidence

Scheier *et al* found that optimistic people take a problem-solving approach, make more plans and use approach-oriented coping, leading to more creativity and goal achievement, which contributes to higher happiness.[62] Optimist individuals, when faced with circumstances that are beyond their control, tend to accept their situations, bestowing a greater sense of peace. In a meta-analysis, it was found that optimism was positively related to indicators of well-being (e.g., happiness), and negatively related to indicators of illness (e.g., anxiety).

The 'Coping Optimism Resources Effect' (CORE) model suggests that optimism impacts psychological well-being. Individuals with higher well-being are likely to use problem-focused coping strategies which may contribute to higher happiness. Broaden-and-build theory may also be used to explain the relationship between optimism and happiness. An optimistic attitude contributes to more frequent experiences of positive affect. Positive emotions such as optimism can help in broadening one's cognitive abilities, leading to higher creativity and

---

62   Scheier, Carver & Bridges, 2001

problem-solving approaches. These enhanced cognitive abilities may lead to higher resilience, social support, knowledge and skills, which may contribute to enhanced fulfilment and happiness.

The following flow chart shows the optimism cycle (how optimism contributes to happiness):

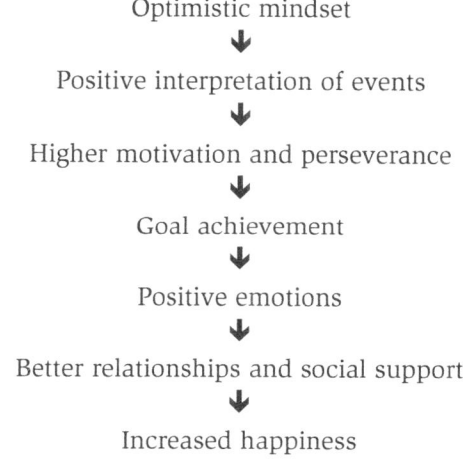

Optimistic mindset
⬇
Positive interpretation of events
⬇
Higher motivation and perseverance
⬇
Goal achievement
⬇
Positive emotions
⬇
Better relationships and social support
⬇
Increased happiness

Cultivating optimism

Reflecting on things you are grateful for may shift your focus from negative to positive aspects of your life, and keeping a gratitude journal may be help you foster greater optimism. During times of difficulties, remind yourself of your previous successes and stay focused on your path of goal achievement. Challenging your negative thoughts and beliefs with more positive perspectives can help in enhancing optimism levels. Focusing on explanatory styles of negative events may give you insights into your patterns or tendencies, and recognizing these patterns may encourage you to challenge them or replace them with more optimistic explanations for negative events. Spending more time with optimistic and supportive people can encourage you to apply problem-solving coping methods and to persist in challenges.

Personal vignette

I always used an optimistic explanatory style when my kids came up short in certain areas. I never thought that such failures were due to attitude, lack of sincerity or similar reasons; I attributed them primarily to more situational factors, and as a result my kids never became despondent. I attribute contextual factors to some of my own failures too – and so, with the unwavering support of family, friends and colleagues, I am able to maintain my optimism.

A brief activity to cultivate optimism

Invite two or three friends or colleagues to engage in a brief activity on optimism. Agree a time and duration for the activity and share the agenda with all the participants in advance. In the beginning of the activity, briefly share some thoughts and ideas about the relationship between optimism and happiness. Encourage everyone to reflect on the positive aspects of their lives, and ask them to write at least three of these positive aspects down. After everyone has done this, ask them to identify at least one optimistic thought or belief related to their lives. Invite them to share their insights, observations and changes in emotional states due to the activity, and encourage them to continue the activity on their own to feel more optimistic in their lives.

Reflective questions

1. Recall a time when you experienced a shift from pessimism to optimism. What triggered that shift? What did you learn from it?
2. What can you do to cultivate a better sense of optimism?
3. What is the relationship between optimism and happiness?
4. What are the sources of your optimism?
5. What did you learn from Marcus's story?

References and further reading

Alarcon, G. M., Bowling, N. A., & Khazon, S. (2013) *Great Expectations: A meta-analytic examination of optimism and hope. Personality and Individual Differences*, 54(7), 821-827.

Brissette, I., Scheier, M. F., & Carver, C. S. (2002) The role of optimism in social network development, coping, and psychological adjustment during a life transition. *Journal of Personality and Social Psychology*, 82(1), 102.

Carver, C. S., & Scheier, M. F. (2001) *On the Self-regulation of Behavior*. Cambridge University Press.

Carver, C. S., & Scheier, M. F. (2014) Dispositional optimism. *Trends in Cognitive Sciences*, 18(6), 293-299.

Dumitrache, C. G., Windle, G., & Rubio Herrera, R. (2015) Do social resources explain the relationship between optimism and life satisfaction in community-dwelling older people? Testing a multiple mediation model. *Journal of Happiness Studies*, 16, 633-654.

Genç, E., & Arslan, G. (2021) Optimism and dispositional hope to promote college students' subjective well-being in the context of the COVID-19 pandemic. *Journal of Positive School Psychology*, 5(2), 87-96.

Puig-Perez, S., Cano-Lopez, I., Martínez, P., Kozusznik, M. W., Alacreu-Crespo, A., Pulopulos, M. M., ... & Kożusznik, B. (2024) Optimism as a protective factor against the psychological impact of COVID-19 pandemic through its effects on perceived stress and infection stress anticipation. *Current Psychology*, 43(9), 8542-8556.

Reizer, A., Munk, Y., & Frankfurter, L. K. (2022) Laughing all the way to the lockdown: On humor, optimism, and well-being during COVID-19. *Personality and Individual Differences*, 184, 111164.

Scheier, M. F., & Carver, C. S. (1985) Optimism, coping, and health: assessment and implications of generalized outcome expectancies. *Health Psychology*, 4(3), 219.

Scheier, M. F., & Carver, C. S. (1992) Effects of optimism on psychological and physical well-being: Theoretical overview and empirical update. *Cognitive Therapy and Research*, 16(2), 201-228.

Scheier, M. F., Carver, C. S., & Bridges, M. W. (2001). Optimism, pessimism, and psychological well-being. In E. C. Chang (Ed.), *Optimism & pessimism: Implications for theory, research, and practice* (pp. 189–216). American Psychological Association.

Schimschal, S. E., Visentin, D., Kornhaber, R., & Cleary, M. (2022) Achieving long-term goals amidst uncertainty: an integrative model for the psychological resources of grit. *The Journal of Continuing Education in Nursing*, 53(8), 355-363.

Seligman, M. E. P. (1998). *Learned Optimism*. Pocket Books.

Smith, J. A., Newman, K. M., Marsh, J., & Keltner, D. (Eds) (2020) *The Gratitude Project: How the science of thankfulness can rewire our brains for resilience, optimism, and the greater good*. New Harbinger Publications.

Vos, L. M., Habibović, M., Nyklíček, I., Smeets, T., & Mertens, G. (2021) Optimism, mindfulness, and resilience as potential protective factors for the mental health consequences of fear of the coronavirus. *Psychiatry Research*, 300, 113927.

Yıldırım, M., & Cicek, I. (2022) Optimism and pessimism mediate the association between parental coronavirus anxiety and depression among healthcare professionals in the era of COVID-19. *Psychology, Health & Medicine*, 27(9), 1898-1906.

P

Chapter 16:
Playfulness

"Play keeps us vital and alive. It gives us an enthusiasm for life that is irreplaceable."

Lucia Capacchione

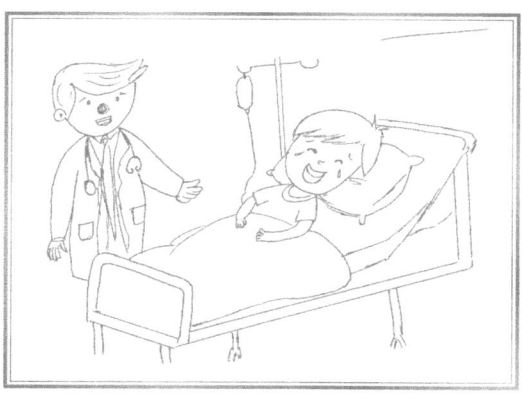

Have you ever noticed how a child's laughter can brighten up a whole room? What if I told you that the secret to happiness might be hidden in those carefree giggles? When we are playful, we try to lighten the atmosphere by picking up cues from our surroundings and using them to say or do something interesting for everyone. Playfulness is the natural tendency to frame (or reframe) a situation in such a way as to provide ourselves and others with amusement, humour, and/or entertainment. Playfulness can enrich both personal and professional lives.

Playfulness can have a lasting impact, bringing ongoing joy, creativity and unexpected insights that transcend time and context. David Love has found this to be true:

Once upon a time there was a young boy who would often be found playfully sketching bizarre creatures and objects. He enjoyed playing with crazy connections and the sketching evolved into the creation of cartoons which highlighted the absurd in the everyday.

He's a leadership coach now, and he encourages clients to approach serious issues with a playful mindset. He creates cartoons about the challenges people face, as well as encouraging them to sketch their own humorous images about the absurdities of organizational life. One client wanted to adopt a coaching style of management, so he drew a cartoon about the client's thoughts on the team's potential reactions.

Playing with the creation of the cartoon helped him clarify the questions he might ask to better serve his client. Immersing himself in a blissful state of flow and losing track of time as he sketched made him happy. And enabling his client to use humour to generate insights about how they could introduce a different management style made them happy. Occasionally he worries that his cartoons are too ephemeral – however, he is pleased when clients make continued use of his or their images, sometimes many months later.

He finds playful collaborations with clients, even about the most serious issues, brings them learning and joy. It provides a new way of seeing a topic – much needed, given that their usual ways of tackling things have not worked. Integrating playfulness and cartooning into his own reflective practice strengthens his service to others – and he feels more authentic than ever in his work. Wielding the pen contributes to him feeling whole.

For years he has also created cartoons for friends and family showing playful images of them in absurd situations. Now in his mid-seventies, the boy (for he is still growing up) plans a posthumous art exhibition at his own wake. Encountering his cartoons, people will laugh anew, creating fresh ripples of happiness – a counterpoint to the sadness that will (hopefully) surround such an event.

How playfully absurd is that!?

David's story beautifully illustrates how playfulness can transform the way we approach challenges, fostering creativity and joy. By integrating playfulness into our work and lives, we can unlock new perspectives and create meaningful connections with others.

Playfulness and happiness

Playfulness is related to experiences of pleasure and positive emotions. It enables us to keep an open mind, and to more easily find solutions to our problems. It generates more creative ideas for solving problems, leading to enhanced positive emotions. According to happiness expert Barabara Fredrickson, playfulness can help us to experience more joy and has the ability to build one's intellectual, physical and social skills.[63] A playful attitude enhances interactions among people, leading to reductions in stress and apprehension, and increased happiness. Playfulness helps us to cope in distressing situations, and it may also help in maintaining a good mood in those distressing situations.

---

63   Fredrickson, 2010

Scientific evidence

In one experimental study, it was found that all playfulness interventions had positive effects on well-being.[64] In another study with a sample of participants ranging from 50 to 98 years old, playfulness was positively related to life satisfaction and different domains of well-being.[65] In another study, from Australia, it was found that playfulness was significantly related to several different indicators of well-being.[66]

Playful individuals experience lower stress levels and more frequently apply positive coping strategies than their less playful counterparts. They also use fewer negative, avoidant and escape-oriented coping strategies, such as self-blaming. Playful individuals see themselves as capable of managing distress, which leads to adaptive and supportive coping outcomes. The use of positive stressor-focused coping reduces stress and leads to higher life satisfaction and well-being. Playfulness is also linked to better psychological functioning, finding joy in learning experiences, and a greater likelihood of reaching states of flow leading to enhanced happiness.

The following flowchart shows how playfulness enhances happiness:

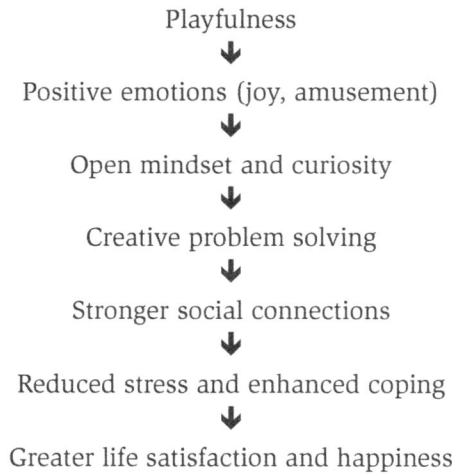

Playfulness
↓
Positive emotions (joy, amusement)
↓
Open mindset and curiosity
↓
Creative problem solving
↓
Stronger social connections
↓
Reduced stress and enhanced coping
↓
Greater life satisfaction and happiness

---

64   Proyer *et al.*, 2021
65   Brauer, Stumpf & Proyer, 2024
66   Farley, Kennedy-Behr & Brown, 2021

Cultivating playfulness

Surround yourself with people who have playful energy. In a playful environment, there is a greater chance of you being more playful. Paying full attention to tasks may help in being playful in some situations. Involving yourself fully in the tasks and interactions with which you are engaged may give opportunities to be playful, and to notice and share something interesting for everyone. Add elements of playfulness to your environment, such as at your desk/workstation, in your car and at home. Adopting a curious mindset while interacting with others can impact playfulness positively, and spending time playing with or simply observing kids and pets can also bring out your own playfulness. Foster a culture of playfulness at work by encouraging light-heartedness in your workplace environment.

The following flowchart shows how to cultivate playfulness:

Set an intention to be playful
⬇
Observe playful people around you
⬇
Engage fully in conversations and tasks
⬇
Add elements of fun to your environment
⬇
Spend time with children, pets or nature
⬇
Use humour to reframe situations
⬇
Celebrate small moments of playfulness

Personal vignette

When talking on the phone, I can sometimes be quite playful. For many years, I would speak playfully with certain people and not with others. But I eventually realized that there was potential to be playful in almost all conversations. I also found that setting an intention to be playful helps greatly to achieve it in different situations. Joyful memories are a big help; interactions with my old school and college friends are always playful, positive experiences.

A brief activity for cultivating playfulness

As a family, make a plan to do something playful at the weekend – each person should try to showcase their unique or silly talents. Gather everyone together in a common area and decide on the time for your performances. Talents on show might include singing, dancing, funny acts, storytelling or whatever the family member might like to try – as long as it's playful and/or silly. They can use props for their performances, and you can encourage them to make groups if they so wish. Each member of the group takes a turn presenting their talent. Celebrate all participants with cheers, high fives, or small rewards to add to the joy generated. This idea could also be used at work to bring some playfulness into your work environment.

Reflective questions

1. Recall your interactions with people who have a tendency to be playful. How did those interactions affect you and others?
2. What beliefs or fears hold you back from being playful while interacting with other people?
3. What activities and environments bring out the playfulness in you?
4. How can you be more interested in tasks and interactions that you already like?
5. How can you bring more playfulness into your work life?
6. How can you bring more playfulness into your family life?
7. What did you learn from David's story?

References and further reading

Barnett, L. A. (2007) The nature of playfulness in young adults. *Pers. Individ. Dif.* 43, 949–958. doi: 10.1016/j.paid.2007.02.018

Brauer, K., Stumpf, H. S. C., & Proyer, R. T. (2024) Playfulness in middle-and older age: Testing associations with life satisfaction, character strengths, and flourishing. *Aging & Mental Health*, 28(11), 1540-1549.

Chang, P. J., Qian, X., & Yarnal, C. (2013) Using playfulness to cope with psychological stress: taking into account both positive and negative emotions. *International Journal of Play*, 2(3), 273-296.

Farley, A., Kennedy-Behr, A., & Brown, T. (2021) An investigation into the relationship between playfulness and well-being in Australian adults: An exploratory study. *OTJR: Occupation, Participation and Health*, 41(1), 56-64.

Fredrickson, B. (2010) *Positivity: Groundbreaking research to release your inner optimist and thrive*. Simon and Schuster.

Hart, T., & Holmes, R. M. (2022) Exploring the connection between adult playfulness and emotional intelligence. *Journal of Play in Adulthood*, 4(1), 28-51.

Kiverstein, J., & Miller, M. (2023) Playfulness and the meaningful life: an active inference perspective. *Neuroscience of Consciousness*, 2023(1), niad024.

Magnuson, C. D., & Barnett, L. A. (2013) The playful advantage: How playfulness enhances coping with stress. *Leisure Sciences*, 35(2), 129-144.

Proyer, R. T., Gander, F., Brauer, K., & Chick, G. (2021) Can playfulness be stimulated? A randomised placebo-controlled online playfulness intervention study on effects on trait playfulness, well-being, and depression. *Applied Psychology: Health and Well-Being*, 13(1), 129-151.

Proyer, R.T. (2017) A new structural model for the study of adult playfulness: Assessment and exploration of an understudied individual differences variable. *Personality and Individual Differences*, 108, 113–122.

Rodríguez-Ardura, I., & Meseguer-Artola, A. (2021) Flow experiences in personalised e-learning environments and the role of gender and academic performance. *Interactive Learning Environments*, 29(1), 59-82.

Tandler, N., Schilling-Friedemann, S., Frazier, L. D., Sendatzki, R., & Proyer, R. T. (2024) New insights into the contributions of playfulness to dealing with stress at work: Correlates of self- and peer-rated playfulness and coping strategies. *New Ideas in Psychology*, 75, 101109.

Q

Chapter 17:
Quiet

"Silence is a source of great strength."

Lao Tzu

When was the last time you truly listened to silence?

In the gentle embrace of quiet moments, we can discover a hidden source of happiness that nourishes our mind, body and soul. Quiet moments are those periods of time that allow us to experience calmness, stillness, contemplation and reflection. They are often characterized by an absence of external distractions, which helps us to turn our focus inward and be mindful. In today's fast-paced world, we need to plan for having quiet moments. They can be short, lasting just a few minutes, or they might last a full day. Quiet moments are an essential part of our perception of the world, and they help us to find meaning in our lives.

Faced with the rush of everyday life, finding these quiet moments is difficult and they are easy to overlook. Technology surrounds us, and we are constantly bombarded with noise. But if we pause and acknowledge the stillness, we may find that happiness is there waiting for us. Life makes quiet moments available to us, but we need to learn to embrace them, and we also need to plan ahead in order to create more of them for ourselves.

Finding moments of quiet can be transformative. Sarah Leach captures beautifully how quiet time not only helps her de-stress but also brings joy, clarity and a sense of happiness:

I have always needed the quiet to de-stress, still my mind and recharge my energy levels. The cacophony of modern life can be overwhelming at times, and the continuous barrage of information and stimuli can leave me feeling drained and on edge. In such a world, finding moments of quiet has been essential for my well-being and allowed me to find joy, fun and happiness in the small things. For me enjoying quiet is the antidote to stiff shoulders and a sore neck, and it allows me to find my smile again.

There are three specific experiences that bring me quiet on a regular basis. First, I love to potter in the kitchen long before the rest of the house stirs. This quiet is my favourite time of day, happily preparing and getting ready for the day ahead, sorting and organizing with no interruptions, other than the light changing and the birds waking.

Secondly, when I'm on my own, I often drive with no radio or audiobook playing. Just me, my own thoughts and the road ahead. I feel society's pressure of filling every moment with something useful such as listening to a podcast on the latest leadership trend while driving to pick my daughter up from school. But this doesn't make me happy. Driving, quietly, allows the events of the day to settle, creating mental space for me to embrace what is next to come.

I find happiness on my daily walk in nature, with only the birdsong and the wind in the trees for company. Again, I rarely listen to anything, just try and find the quiet. Recently, my husband and I embarked on a seven-mile walk where we didn't encounter a single soul. The winter fog had descended, shrouding the landscape in a thick, silent blanket. We couldn't see the view, but that didn't matter. The gentle sound of our steps, and the profound silence that surrounded us, were enough. We stopped and listened to the stillness, and I almost caught my breath at how perfect it was. In that moment, I felt truly happy.

Sarah's experience shows us that moments of quiet are not just a luxury – they are essential for our well-being. Whether it's in the kitchen, on the road or in nature, taking time to embrace stillness allows us to recharge, reset and reconnect with ourselves. In a world filled with noise and distractions that constantly demands our attention, these quiet moments can serve as an antidote to chaos, and a powerful tool for finding peace and happiness.

Quiet and happiness

Silence calms the mind and body and reduces anxiety and stress. Relaxed minds lead to better opportunities to reflect on whatever is going on, and to make adjustments in different areas of our lives. These adjustments enhance peace of mind. Being in silence for some time allows us to connect with ourselves and become aware of our concerns, which sometimes don't come to our conscious awareness in the normal routine of doing and rushing. This awareness can motivate us to do something about these concerns, leading to satisfaction and fulfilment.

In quiet moments, we also become more aware of our blessings and the positive things in life, leading to greater appreciation and gratitude. Moments spent in silence also enhance the chances of us discovering new ideas, insights and solutions, leading to better management of problems and helping us achieve our goals. During quiet moments, we can focus mindfully on the present moment, which reduces worries and increases joy in daily experiences. Quiet moments shared with loved ones can enhance our understanding of each other, improving our relationships and developing deeper connections. Quiet moments encourage self-care and promote happiness, and they may also enhance self-acceptance and self-esteem.

The hustle and bustle of life leaves little room for stillness. This story from Fatima Hussain shows how small, quiet, simple moments can restore our sense of calm and clarity:

I think about our everyday environment and how it can affect us in ways we don't realise. Our day-to-day lives are filled with so much noise. This noise seeps through to the depths of our minds. At work we hustle, trying to climb the corporate ladder; meetings, discussions, calls, networking, socializing and bonding with the team; all while ensuring that project deadlines are met. At home, we fulfil our designated roles, making sure that household tasks are complete, while spending time with family and fulfilling obligations. To add to all of that, our urban environment is filled with noise pollution, traffic, construction, people arguing on the streets and so much more. All of this noise creates the perfect recipe for dysregulation within our nervous system – creating anxiety, stress, frustration and more.

When the noise of life starts to get intense, I pause. Take a deep breath. Find a quiet spot and close the door. Plug in my noise-cancelling headphones. Reclaim calm, clarity and connection with myself. I pay attention to what my senses are seeing, hearing, feeling and smelling. I step outside and look at the sky for a few minutes. Admire the shade of blue, the shape of the clouds, the birds that fly across the vast space. At night, I stare at the moon and the stars. How they light up the sky. Appreciate the beauty of the things I see around me. This is my happy place. This is what helps regulate me.

I relax and seek solace in activities that add to my happiness. For me, that's reading a chapter or two of a book, watching an episode of a favourite show, or simply sitting with my thoughts. Just a few moments all to myself. I automatically feel relaxed and energized to enter the hustle once again. Cutting through the noise to the quiet moments is my happy place.

> *And in these small moments of peace, I find myself being centred.*
> *In these times of quiet, I find happiness that recharges me and keeps*
> *me going for when I must return to the daily hustle and grind. And*
> *once the moment has passed, I tuck it within myself and step out into*
> *the noise to strive and thrive towards my goals once more.*

Fatima's story shows us that by intentionally seeking out moments of quiet for the self, we can recharge and return to our goals with renewed focus and energy. So, next time you feel overwhelmed, take a pause, find your calm, and let it guide you forward.

Scientific evidence

In his article *Solitude: Embracing the Quiet Power of Time Alone*, Mark Adams explains that quiet moments are fundamental to maintaining our emotional and psychological balance.[67] Quiet moments satisfy our need for autonomy, competence and relatedness, leading to psychological well-being. In a study by Asselineau *et al*, it was found that moments of silence can serve as emotion regulators and may help individuals and organizations in individual and collective decision making.[68] They recommended that managers and leaders exploit the power of silence to make the workplace and the world a better place for everyone.

In four studies, Weinstein *et al* used complementary methods – cross-sectional, daily diary keeping and experimental designs – to explore the phenomenon of silence.[69] They found that intrinsically motivated silence was felt with more positive affect and less negative affect, and that relationships were closer and more satisfying during intrinsically motivated moments of silence. Silence is now acknowledged to be a significant part of healthy human development and well-being. Researchers suggest that solitude and silence are linked to profound personal outcomes. including the discovery of new, expansive ways of knowing oneself and the world.[70]

---

67   Adams, 2024
68   Asselineau, Grolleau & Mzoughi, 2024
69   Weinstein *et al.*, 2024
70   Naor & Mayseless, 2020

Cultivating quiet

You can create quiet moments by reducing the noise in your environment, or by moving to spaces that naturally have no noise. To enhance quiet moments in your life, make it a part of your everyday routine to find some time to sit in silence and explore the benefits it can bring. It can be any time of your choice. Remove devices and distractions from the space you want to use for quiet moments. Perhaps add a ritual around your quiet time, such as lighting a candle, having a cup of tea, deep breathing, taking a slow walk or whatever works for you. Such rituals will signal to the mind that it is time to relax and embrace stillness. You may want to journal, express gratitude or read. During your quiet moments, you might also use creative means to express your thoughts such as drawing, mind maps, visualizations or doodling.

To begin with, you might need to learn to embrace moments of stillness without giving in to the feeling that you need to fill them with activities. Just be there, even if it's only for a short time. Gradually, you'll start to enjoy it more and more, and you'll begin to see the benefits for your mental state. By incorporating some of the ideas discussed above and creating intentional pauses during your day, you'll enjoy clarity, deeper peace and happiness.

Nature and solitude can help to enhance the quiet moments in your life. You could even attend silent retreats and workshops to deepen your personal practice of mindfulness and observe its impact on you. Mindfulness offers a proven route to cultivate quiet moments and a focused mindset that allows you to manage stress, make thoughtful decisions, and manage your emotions, leading to enhanced happiness and well-being.

Personal vignette

When I wake each morning, I just walk and connect with myself. These quiet moments give me opportunities to reflect on my relationships and challenges, and I often come up with new ideas for solving or improving them. Quiet moments also inspire me to exercise and meditate more, in order to enhance my physical and mental health. As you move through your day, seek out these moments and allow them to nourish your mind, body and spirit.

A brief activity for cultivating quiet

Find a quiet and comfortable space where nothing will distract and disturb you. Sit in a relaxed position and take several deep breaths. Spend some time – five minutes or so – just observing your thoughts, emotions and physical sensations without any judgement. Feel the calmness and embrace the stillness. Afterwards, reflect on the experience and how it made you feel, and notice its effects on your peace of mind and happiness. Acknowledge any insights and feelings that emerged during the session. If you want, you can share your experience with your loved one. You may decide on a time and space to indulge in quiet moments in the future.

Reflective questions

1. How do quiet moments help you to enhance your happiness?
2. What creative ways will help you to stay engaged during your quiet moments?
3. Have you had quiet moments when silence brought you ideas and joy?
4. What small adjustments might help you to fully embrace the quiet moments in your life?
5. How might quiet moments help you in your relationships with your loved ones?
6. What might be the most convenient time and space for embracing quiet moments for you?
7. What did you learn from Sarah's story?
8. What did you learn from Fatima's story?

References and further reading

Adams, M. (2024) *Solitude: Embracing the quiet power of time alone.* Society for Personality and Social Psychology. Available at: https://spsp.org/news/character-and-context-blog/adams-solitude-embracing-quiet-power-time-alone (accessed May 2025).

Asselineau, A., Grolleau, G., & Mzoughi, N. (2024) Quiet environments and the intentional practice of silence: Toward a new perspective in the analysis of silence in organizations. *Industrial and Organizational Psychology*, 17(3), 326-340.

Detwiler, L. (2017) *Sometimes the Best Moments in Life Are The Quietest.* HuffPost. Available at: www.huffpost.com/entry/sometimes-the-best-moments-in-life-are-the-quietest_b_5963664de4b0 85e766b51438 (accessed May 2025).

Kramer, G. (2007) *Insight Dialogue: The interpersonal path to freedom*. Shambhala Publications.

Ling, S. (2024) *Appreciating the quiet moments: Finding joy in the ordinary. Youth Are Awesome*. Available at: https://youthareawesome.com/appreciating-the-quiet-moments-finding-joy-in-the-ordinary/ (accessed May 2025).

Naor, L., & Mayseless, O. (2020) The wilderness solo experience: A unique practice of silence and solitude for personal growth. *Frontiers in Psychology*, 11, 547067.

Passmore, J. (2022) Mindfulness in coaching: Being the observer. *Coaching Practiced*, 359-361.

Pfeifer, E., Pothmann, K., Claaßen, S., & Wittmann, M. (2023) Increased relaxation, less boredom, and a faster passage of time during a period of silence in the forest. *Progress in Brain Research*, 277, 157-180.

Røgild-Müller, L. (2022) SILENCE: Capturing the feeling of inner quietude. Integrative *Psychological and Behavioral Science*, 56(1), 133-162.

Siegel, R. D. (2010) *The Mindfulness Solution: Everyday practices for everyday problems*. Guilford Press.

Stanier, M. B. (2016) *The Coaching Habit: Say less, ask more and change the way you lead forever*. Box of Crayons Press.

Weinstein, N., Nguyen, T. V., Adams, M., & Knee, C. R. (2024) Intimate sounds of silence: its motives and consequences in romantic relationships. *Motivation and Emotion*, 1-26.

R

Chapter 18:
Relaxation

"The time to relax is when you don't have time for it."
Sydney J. Harris

In the chaos of life, relaxation often appears like a distant island – visible yet unreachable. But what if that island is closer than we think, hidden in simple moments we often overlook?

Relaxation is the conscious effort to reduce mental and physical tension. It helps calm the mind, reduce stress, reduce fatigue and increase happiness. The regular practice of relaxation may help to enhance our physical and mental health. All the traditions in the world have created rituals or techniques that may help with relaxation, and psychologists too have developed their own approaches. In this age of constant pressure and challenge, it is important to learn some relaxation techniques to reduce anxiety and stress and live a peaceful and happy life.

> **Relaxation often finds its way into our lives in unexpected ways, as beautifully illustrated by this personal account on the importance of unwinding from Robert Biswas-Diener:**
>
> *I'll be honest: relaxation snuck up on me. I come from a family of non-relaxers. We are, instead, high achievers. My father was a highly regarded scientist. My mother earned her second doctorate in her fifties. Both of my older sisters are university professors. Even our vacations feel like a high-octane to-do list: how many beaches, snorkelling spots and restaurants can we cram into a single tropical holiday?*
>
> *In this context, I will be the first to admit that – for years – I filled my evenings and weekends with work. I love designing new projects, learning new skills, and getting caught up on tasks. Even when I did schedule recreation, it was of the skiing-all-day or take-a-long-hike variety. My leisure time always felt as if it were every bit as much about accomplishment as my workdays.*
>
> *All that changed in 2018, when I travelled to Florence and Venice. Like many visitors, I was enchanted by the architecture, which rekindled my love of drawing. I have some natural talent but had put away my pens and pencils for decades to focus on the more serious pursuits of work and family. While in Italy, however, I did a few brief sketches of the Duomo and other buildings.*
>
> *I immediately realized many things: drawing each day satisfied my need for learning and improving; it was a mindfulness activity that offered me the daily experience of flow; it was a critical opportunity to focus on process rather than outcome; and – most importantly – it boosted my well-being. Now, I prioritize at least a half hour of drawing each morning and feel better when I do so.*

> *It turns out that my instincts align with the research on relaxation. Studies reveal that mental and physical relaxation are associated with lower stress levels in general and at work. This makes intuitive sense since relaxation is, by definition, an absence of stress. Often, off-the-clock relaxation allows people to mentally disengage from work which restores their psychological resources for when they next work.*
>
> *Finally, I came to understand that daily artwork was not selfish. By prioritizing my well-being, I generally feel stronger, more resilient, and more capable of contributing to others.*

Robert's journey serves as a powerful reminder that prioritizing relaxation not only enhances our own well-being; it also strengthens our capacity to support and connect with others.

Relaxation and happiness

Relaxation reduces stress and anxiety, which helps in enhancing happiness. A relaxed mind is less worried. less agitated and can see things clearly. This helps us to solve our problems and find solutions to reach our goals, generating satisfaction and fulfilment. Relaxation promotes the release of positive chemicals, leading to positive feelings of joy and contentment. It helps with better sleep, which boosts health and overall happiness. And it helps to release muscle tension and improves the immune system, contributing to overall well-being. A relaxed state of mind also improves empathy, understanding and patience, leading to better relationships with other people – a key driver of human happiness.

With a relaxed mind, we can better appreciate what we have, and express gratitude to others for helping us resolve our issues and achieve our goals. Such feelings of appreciation and gratitude lead to satisfaction and fulfilment in life. A relaxed mind is a more mindful mind, better able to focus on the present moment – reducing worries and negative thought patterns. A relaxed mind also has a higher tendency for self-acceptance, which contributes to well-being.

Scientific evidence

In a recent experimental study, Tapeh *et al* found that Jacobson's Progressive Muscle Relaxation (JPMR) had a positive effect on reducing anxiety and enhancing happiness in elderly people.[71] They recommended developing training programmes and allocating time to non-pharmacological treatments such as JPMR to help elderly people become happier and healthier. In a similar study conducted with students, researchers suggested that progressive muscle relaxation techniques should be used to help students manage their stress and enhance happiness.[72] One more study found that our happiest moments are closely related to leisure time, leisure space and leisure activities.[73] The researchers suggested that, by participating in leisure activities, people detach themselves from work and relax, recovering from the heavy pressures of modern life.

Crowley *et al* explored differences in mindfulness, happiness and perceived anxiety in a sample of college students before and after taking a meditation course.[74] They found that, after the meditation course, the students had increased average subjective happiness and mindfulness attention awareness scores, and that mindfulness scores increased and anxiety decreased more for students in the meditation class compared to students in the psychosocial class. In a meta-analysis on physical relaxation for occupational stress in healthcare workers, the researchers found that physical relaxation may help reduce occupational stress in this group.[75] It was also suggested that yoga is particularly effective and offers the convenience of online delivery. Employers could consider implementing these methods into workplace wellness programmes.

Cultivating relaxation

There are many different techniques for relaxation, depending on the context, and you can learn which method suits you and your context best. A good way to incorporate relaxation into your life is to

---

71 Tapeh *et al.*, 2024
72 Bostani *et al.*, 2020
73 Liu & Da, 2020
74 Crowley, Kapitula & Munk, 2022
75 Zhang *et al.*, 2021

establish a relaxation routine. To do this, you can explore a range of methods for yourself. Some examples of relaxation techniques are deep breathing, meditation, stretching, progressive muscle relaxation, or guided meditation through apps such as Calm or Headspace. Engaging in enjoyable hobbies such as painting, crafting, writing, drawing, singing, playing a musical instrument, walking or swimming can help to relax the body and mind, as can reading books, listening to music, decluttering your environment and spending time in nature. Reducing screen time, especially before going to bed, helps promote sound sleep and better relaxation.

It is important to acknowledge that there are certain limitations and barriers that we simply cannot change, overcome or solve in life. Accepting these reduces our worries and enhances our ability to relax. Focusing on what we have rather than what we lack enhances our gratitude and appreciation, leading to satisfaction and fulfilment. Sharing our concerns with family and friends also helps us to relax. Sometimes, just being in the moment can lead to relaxation.

Personal vignette

Whenever I meditate to relax my mind, it makes me feel calm. I use deep breathing and body scans, as well as some favourite relaxation techniques. After meditation, my interactions with others are smoother. My mind and body are relaxed. Meditation helps me to clarify what I want to achieve, and it gives me the confidence to pursue my goals and motivate others to do the same. Such conversations inspire all of us to do the best we can.

A brief activity for cultivating relaxation

Sit in a comfortable position, in a space free from distractions and noise, and close your eyes. Focus on your breath and experience the inhalation and exhalation of the air. Next, focus your attention on the top of your head. Start shifting your attention slowly downwards, moving down your body until you reach to the tips of your toes. Then move your attention back from your toes to the top of your head. Keep moving your attention and observing, without judgement, what sensations you notice. Do five rounds of this, scanning your whole body slowly and mindfully. After the five rounds, bring your attention back to your normal breath and, after some time, open your eyes. Feel the calmness and peace in your mind and body.

Reflective questions

1. What activities, rituals and environments do you find the most relaxing?
2. How has relaxation helped you in the past? How can you use that learning in the future?
3. What distractions and habitual patterns affect your ability to relax and what can you do to manage those distractions and patterns?
4. How can you insert small relaxation doses into your everyday life?
5. What can you learn from kids to enhance relaxation in your life?
6. What activities have you found that don't help much in relaxing your mind?
7. What did you learn from Robert's story?

References and further reading

Arora, S., & Bhattacharjee, J. (2008) Modulation of immune responses in stress by Yoga. *International Journal of Yoga*, 1(2), 45-55.

Bostani, S., Rambod, M., Irani, P. S., & Torabizadeh, C. (2020) Comparing the effect of progressive muscle relaxation exercise and support group therapy on the happiness of nursing students: A randomized clinical trial study. *International Journal of Africa Nursing Sciences*, 13, 100218.

Can, Y. S., Iles-Smith, H., Chalabianloo, N., Ekiz, D., Fernández-Álvarez, J., Repetto, C., Riva, G., & Ersoy, C. (2020) How to relax in stressful situations: A smart stress reduction system. *Healthcare*, 8(2), 100.

Capps, D. (2009) Relaxed bodies, emancipated minds, and dominant calm. *Journal of Religion and Health*, 48, 368-380.

Crowley, C., Kapitula, L. R., & Munk, D. (2022) Mindfulness, happiness, and anxiety in a sample of college students before and after taking a meditation course. *Journal of American College Health*, 70(2), 493-500.

Davis, M., Eshelman, E. R., & McKay, M. (2008) *The Relaxation and Stress Reduction Workbook*. New Harbinger Publications.

Debellemaniere, E., Gomez-Merino, D., Erblang, M., Dorey, R., Genot, M., Perreaut-Pierre, E., Pisani, A., Rocco, L., Sauvet, F., Léger, D., Rabat, A., & Chennaoui, M. (2018) Using relaxation techniques to improve sleep during naps. *Industrial Health*, 56(3), 220-227.

Drigas, A., & Mitsea, E. (2021) Metacognition, Stress-Relaxation Balance & Related Hormones. *Int. J. Recent Contributions Eng. Sci. IT*, 9(1), 4-16.

Feldman, G., Greeson, J., & Senville, J. (2010) Differential effects of mindful breathing, progressive muscle relaxation, and loving-kindness meditation on decentering and negative reactions to repetitive thoughts. *Behaviour Research and Therapy*, 48(10), 1002-1011.

Jain, S., Shapiro, S. L., Swanick, S., Roesch, S. C., Mills, P. J., Bell, I., & Schwartz, G. E. (2007) A randomized controlled trial of mindfulness meditation versus relaxation training: Effects on distress, positive states of mind, rumination, and distraction. *Annals of Behavioral Medicine*, 33, 11-21.

Liu, H., & Da, S. (2020) The relationships between leisure and happiness-A graphic elicitation method. *Leisure Studies* 39(1): 111-130.

Merlin, N. M., & Ropyanto, C. B. (2019) The effects of quantum psychological relaxation technique on self-acceptance in patients with breast cancer. *Canadian Oncology Nursing Journal*, 29(4), 232-236.

Ridderinkhof, A., de Bruin, E. I., Brummelman, E., & Bögels, S. M. (2017) Does mindfulness meditation increase empathy? An experiment. *Self and Identity*, 16(3), 251-269.

Tapeh, Z. A., Darvishpour, A., Besharati, F., & Gholami-Chaboki, B. (2024) Effect of Jacobson's Progressive Muscle Relaxation on Anxiety and Happiness of Older Adults in the Nursing Home. *Iranian Journal of Nursing and Midwifery Research*, 29(1), 78-84.

Zhang, M., Murphy, B., Cabanilla, A., & Yidi, C. (2021) Physical relaxation for occupational stress in healthcare workers: A systematic review and network meta-analysis of randomized controlled trials. *Journal of Occupational Health*, 63(1), e12243.

S

Chapter 19:
Savouring

*"Slow down and savour your life's moments.
The simple things are the most beautiful."*

Steve Maraboli

Pause for a moment.

Recall a time when you truly savoured something – a delicious meal, a breathtaking sunset or a heartfelt conversation. How did it feel to be fully present in that moment? Recall when you cooked with family without pressure to achieve anything. Recall when you saw trees, mountains and a clear sky, and felt fresh air. All these experiences belong to savouring.

Fred Bryant and Joseph Veroff define savouring as 'the capacity to attend to, appreciate, and enhance the positive experiences in one's life', and say that 'people have capacities to attend to, appreciate, and enhance the positive experiences in their lives'.[76] Savouring involves thoughts and actions that are aimed at appreciating and amplifying a positive experience. In order to savour, we need to be actively engaged and fully absorbed in what is happening in the moment. We need to have a mindful focus on the pleasurable features of an experience.

Savouring can take three forms, correlating to future, present and past:

1. Anticipating a forthcoming positive event, like graduating from college.

2. Being in the moment, or thinking and doing things to intensify and perhaps prolong a positive event as it occurs, like savouring a good meal.

3. Reminiscing, or looking back at a positive event to rekindle favourable feelings or thoughts, like savouring a great time spent with friends.

Lindsay Oades beautifully illustrates how savouring memories of the past and hopes for the future can bring joy and connection, even in the midst of life's challenges:

I have always been fascinated by time. It has been said that depression is being in the past, anxiety is being in the future and happiness lives in the present. Well-being, like financial wealth, can be considered a trade-off between happiness in the present and happiness in the future.

During COVID-19, my family and I, as residents of Melbourne, Australia, experienced the most days locked down in the world. We had certain hours during the day where we could travel, in my case walk, within a certain distance from our home. For me, as someone who was used to travelling to many places across the world several times a year, this was a dramatic change.

---

76   Bryant & Veroff, 2007

It occurred to me that our lives are made up of travelling not only in space, but also in time. So, since my movements were restricted in space, I decided I would move in time. Each day, through my large network of digital friends, I posted my time travel photos, things from the past, personal (e.g. when I was younger) or when things were different on the anniversary of that day. I also posted things I hoped for in the future, communicated in a visual image and a brief message. So time became the axis of travel, enabling me to connect with others also, and reminisce and be hopeful, despite the physical restraints of the current situation.

I was heartened by the numerous messages I received during and after my long series of time travel photos and stories, with people saying how much it had helped them.

Lindsay's experience serves as a reminder that savouring life's moments – whether by reminiscing about the past, living fully in the present, or imagining the future – can transform even the most challenging times into opportunities for joy, reflection and connection.

Savouring and happiness

Savouring amplifies feelings of pleasure, joy and gratitude, leading to an overall increase in positive emotions. Savouring requires lingering and appreciating the nuances and richness of our experiences, enhancing our overall sense of satisfaction and happiness. Therefore, actively seeking out or savouring positive experiences enhances happiness and satisfaction in life. Becoming absorbed in moments of savouring can also bring us into flow states, leading to reductions in stress and increases in happiness.

Savouring can build personal resources that help people deal with demands and stressors more effectively, thereby minimizing their negative effects on well-being. Savouring experiences with others enriches social connections, leading to more positive relationships. Discussing positive work experiences at home can help us to process the day's events and experience a better work-family facilitation. These better positive relations then contribute to our overall well-being.

For David Tee, the act of cooking for others has become a powerful way to savour life. Here, he shares how the experience has become much more than just preparing a meal:

An enduring source of happiness for me is cooking for family and friends. Arguably, this is the closest act to magic – taking a set of ingredients and transforming them into a spellbinding dish. I hope that my fellow diners and I literally savour the end offering – the meal itself – but this is almost an afterthought for me. A mere bonus. What I truly savour is the entire experience leading up to the moment the food is served: the intent, the planning, the hunting/gathering of the resources, then the actual, purposeful time in the kitchen in the act of preparing and then cooking the ingredients.

So many reasons why I savour this come to mind. I view it as purposeful, focused time – a valued opportunity to decompress after the juggling of priorities throughout the working week. It is also indulgent 'Me time' – my music playlist on too loud. A cheeky glass or two of whatever I fancy ("chef's privilege"). Treasured friends sat around the kitchen island, chatting about whatever we wish. Bliss.

Finally, it aligns to my 'love of learning' signature strength. I am a vegetarian, which has opened my mind to dishes more exotic than I might otherwise have encountered. So it is always a new recipe, rather than a trusted favourite, and may well require detective work in locating obscure ingredients. Fabulous!

Added together, this means that any wider cares and pressures, temporary or enduring, seem to dissipate with the steam from the oven. This feels somehow 'other'. The food is ready when it is ready – no imposed deadline. Let us instead just savour the entire experience.

David's story shows us that savouring is about enjoying the process, not just the outcome. Whether it's cooking, learning, or spending time with loved ones, taking time to savour the experience brings true happiness.

Scientific evidence

According to broaden-and-build theory, positive emotions enhance cognitive abilities leading to enhanced resilience, social support, knowledge and skills.[77] These enhanced resources help in health and fulfilment. Acknowledging and being present and savouring moments can boost resources such as skills, resilience and social support, leading to better health and fulfilment.

Csikszentmihalyi and Larson suggested that the best predictor of daily positive affect may be the absence of alienation from the self.[78] Thus, by being present and avoiding worrying, one can maximize positive affect levels. Many studies have found that practicing savouring can enhance happiness, and there is a large body of empirical evidence that illustrates that savouring promotes positive psychological functioning, including happiness and satisfaction. In a study that used daily diary writing, it was found that savouring is an important mechanism through which we derive happiness from positive events.[79] In a meta-analytic review, it was found that savouring interventions had a positive effect on happiness.[80]

Cultivating savouring

Savouring can be enhanced by being present – by deliberately directing your attention to the present moment, and the pleasant experiences you are having. To become fully absorbed in a moment, avoid distractions and focus only on the positive features of the here-and-now.

Savouring can also be enhanced by communicating and celebrating positive events with others – a strategy known as capitalizing. Sharing positive experiences can be done by talking about an experience or by writing about it. Expressing positive emotions through non-verbal behaviours like laughing, pumping fists in the air and holding hands with loved ones enhances savouring. When something good happens, take time to celebrate it. When others share their positive news, show enthusiasm and respond with a positive comment.

---

77   Fredrickson, 2001
78   Csikszentmihalyi & Larson, 1987
79   Jose, Lim & Bryant, 2012
80   Smith *et al.*, 2014

When you can, engage in what I call 'Positive Mental Time Travel' by vividly remembering or anticipating positive events. Look back at previous positive moments you have experienced and try to savour them, and look ahead to future positive events. Appreciating the fleeting and precious nature of an exciting positive moment may contribute to savouring.

It is possible to pause from the fast-paced aspects of life and add moments of savouring throughout the day. Congratulating yourself on a positive outcome, however big or small, can lead to savouring. With practice, savouring can become a general mindset applied to more and more aspects of your life. We can savour more by counting our blessings.

The following flowchart shows a simple process for savouring in daily life.

Pause
Take a mindful pause in your day

Notice
Pay attention to positive details (sights, sounds, tastes)

Absorb
Stay fully present and immerse yourself in the moment

Express
Share your joy through a smile, a gesture or through words

Reflect
Afterwards, revisit the moment in your mind to prolong
its positive impact

Personal vignette

We are a celebrating family. My daughter will always make a victory sign whenever she achieves something, even if it's only something very minor. She always savours every small success. My wife expresses her happiness with a 'Yay!', helping her to savour a particular moment. Whenever we bring a chocolate for our son, he will clap, hug us and his happiness will be fully visible on his face. So, each in their own way, we fully savour those moments.

A brief activity for cultivating savouring

Find a comfortable and quiet space. Remove all distractions, like mobile phones and computers, and switch off the TV and music. Take a few deep breaths, then close your eyes and try for several minutes to see in your mind's eye all the positive moments you can think of. Touch on each moment lightly, feeling its positivity. When you are ready, bring your focus back to your breath and gently open your eyes. Now write down all the positive moments you thought of and reflect on the sensations you experienced during the activity. Repeat the activity whenever you want to enhance your happiness through savouring.

Reflective questions

1. Think of a recent positive experience that you fully savoured. What factors might have helped you to savour it so fully?

2. Think of a recent positive experience that you didn't fully savour. What might have prevented you from fully savouring it?

3. How can you enhance savouring experiences despite your hectic daily routine?

4. What are some situations that naturally facilitate or encourage savouring for you?

5. What did you learn from Lindsay's story?

6. What did you learn from David's story?

References and further reading

Borelli, J. L., Smiley, P. A., Kerr, M. L., Hong, K., Hecht, H. K., Blackard, M. B., ... & Bond, D. K. (2020) Relational Savoring: An attachment-based approach to promoting interpersonal flourishing. *Psychotherapy*, 57(3), 340.

Bryant, F. B., and Veroff, J. (2007) *Savoring: A new model of positive experience.* Mahwah, NJ: Lawrence Erlbaum Associates.

Csikszentmihalyi, M., & Larson, R. (1987) Validity and reliability of the experience sampling method. *Journal of Nervous and Mental Disease*, 175, 526–536.

Culbertson SS, Mills MJ, Fullagar CJ. (2012) Work engagement and work-family facilitation: making homes happier through positive affective spillover. *Hum. Relat.* 65(9):1155–77.

Fred B. Bryant. (2021) Current Progress and Future Directions for Theory and Research on Savoring. *Frontiers in Psychology*, 12. https://doi.org/10.3389/fpsyg.2021.771698

Fredrickson, B. L. (2001) The role of positive emotions in positive psychology: The broaden-and-build theory of positive emotions. *American Psychologist*, 56(3), 218-226.

Ilies, R., Bono, J. E., & Bakker, A. B. (2024) Crafting well-being: Employees can enhance their own well-being by savoring, reflecting upon, and capitalizing on positive work experiences. *Annual Review of Organizational Psychology and Organizational Behavior*, 11(1), 63-91.

Ilies, R., Wagner, D., Wilson, K., Ceja, L., Johnson, M., DeRue, S., & Ilgen, D. (2017) Flow at work and basic psychological needs: Effects on well-being. *Applied Psychology*, 66(1), 3-24.

Jose, P. E., Bryant, F. B., & Macaskill, E. (2021) Savor now and also reap the rewards later: Amplifying savoring predicts greater uplift frequency over time. *The Journal of Positive Psychology*, 16(6), 738-748.

Jose, P. E., Lim, B. T., & Bryant, F. B. (2012) Does savoring increase happiness? A daily diary study. *The Journal of Positive Psychology*, 7(3), 176-187.

Pitts, M. J., Fanari, A., Cooper, R. A., Jiao, J., & Kim, S. (2023) The Grounded Model of Communication Savoring: Theory Development and Age Cohort Study. *American Journal of Qualitative Research*, 7(3), 139-159.

Quoidbach, J., Berry, E. V., Hansenne, M., & Mikolajczak, M. (2010) Positive emotion regulation and well-being: Comparing the impact of eight savoring and dampening strategies. *Personality and Individual Differences*, 49(5), 368-373.

Smith, J. L., Harrison, P. R., Kurtz, J. L., & Bryant, F. B. (2014) Nurturing the capacity to savor: Interventions to enhance the enjoyment of positive experiences. *The Wiley Blackwell Handbook of Positive Psychological Interventions*, 42-65.

Smith, J. L., Harrison, P. R., Kurtz, J. L., & Bryant, F. B. (2014) Nurturing the capacity to savor: Interventions to enhance the enjoyment of positive experiences. In: A. C. Parks & S. M. Schueller (Eds.), *The Wiley Blackwell Handbook of Positive Psychological Interventions* (pp42-65). Wiley Blackwell.

Sthapit, E., Björk, P., Jiménez-Barreto, J., & Stone, M. J. (2021) Spillover effect, positive emotions and savouring processes: Airbnb guests' perspective. *Anatolia*, 32(1), 33-45.

T

Chapter 20:

Time

> *"The easiest way to increase happiness is to control your use of time. Can you find more time to do the things you enjoy doing?"*
>
> Daniel Kahneman

Time is a precious gift – how we invest, use and manage it shapes our happiness, well-being and satisfaction. And in the modern world, with all its distractions, it has become more important than ever to effectively manage our time if we are to lead a happy and fulfilling life. Actively making time for happiness gives us the feeling that we have more of it.

We manage our time by intentionally planning and making mindful choices about how we spend it across different activities. Time management can also be about prioritizing tasks and activities, and eliminating non-essential activities. Claessens *et al* reviewed thirty-two empirical studies and defined time management as: 'behaviours that aim at achieving an effective use of time while performing certain goal-directed activities.'[81]

> **Time is the ultimate finite resource. In this story, Catherine Steele shares how prioritizing moments of joy and self-care helped her create a more balanced, fulfilling life:**
>
> *Like many of us, my life feels pretty full, and I have multiple roles that I fulfil. I feel fortunate to enjoy the roles I hold, but there are still occasions when time feels pressured. A while ago, I sought support from a health coach as I felt overwhelmed. We discussed what I enjoyed doing – which I found really challenging, as it felt like such a long time since I had felt those feelings! The outcome was I signed up to a yoga course with a weekly one-hour class. A big part of me felt this was crazy, as I was already busy. How was I going to fit this in as well?*
>
> *After the first week, I felt good – calm and joyful. I completed the course, and the benefits were clear: I was making a weekly commitment to myself, and somehow it felt like I had MORE time! I have continued to make my happiness a priority; now this looks like a monthly book club, more yoga and regular scheduled time with family and friends. Our family has a weekly planner purely for the things we have scheduled that bring us joy (we have multiple other planners for all the other tasks!) so we can check that there is a balance.*
>
> *Time is a key factor in happiness, and it is precious. It's not merely about the quantity of time, but how it's spent. By investing time in enriching experiences and nurturing relationships, my happiness increased significantly.*

Time can feel like a burden or a gift, depending on how we use it. Catherine learned that true happiness isn't about having more time; it's about making the most of the time we have.

---

81   Claessens *et al.*, 2007

Time and happiness

Using our time effectively helps us to achieve our goals, leading to enhanced satisfaction and happiness. Effective time management also reduces anxiety and stress – especially that related to wasting time on non-essential things, not doing anything at all, not completing the most important tasks, and leaving things until the last minute. When we use our time for the most important tasks at that point in time, it gives us happiness and fulfilment.

Effective use of time enhances the chances of us doing the things we enjoy. It helps us to plan time for different areas of our lives, and it allows us to feel more fulfilled by investing our time in the right areas. Effective time management also increases productivity, leading to higher levels of achievement and well-being. It enhances happiness, because it encourages a sense of accomplishment discourages anxiety due to procrastination or avoiding tasks. Effective use of time also allows us to create space for relaxation and leisure, further enhancing our happiness. When we learn to enjoy our work, and to make the most of our free time, we end up feeling that our lives as a whole have become much more worthwhile.

Scientific evidence

According to one recent study, effective time management reduces stress while allowing more time for enjoyable activities.[82] Ilona Boniwell and Evgeny Osin found that good use of time results from choosing activities that help people to satisfy their basic needs and are directed at intrinsic goals such as helping other people, establishing relationships, developing oneself and growing as a person, and maintaining health and balance in one's life.[83] Satisfaction of basic needs and the achievement of intrinsic goals lead to higher well-being. They also suggest that providing people with more opportunities to pursue goals that align with their values and intrinsic motivations benefits both the individual and society as a whole.

---

82   Thongri, Seksan & Warintarawej, 2024
83   Boniwell & Osin, 2015

In a recent research review conducted by Dunigan Folk and Elizabeth Dunn, it was found that reducing unpleasant tasks from one's day may be an effective – and underused – strategy for promoting happiness.[84] In a meta-analysis looking at whether time management works, the researchers found that effective time management was related to better job performance, academic achievement and well-being.[85] They also concluded that time management actually enhances well-being to a greater extent than it enhances performance.

Cultivating time

The effective use of time requires knowing your most important and inspiring goals across various domains of life and assessing the key things to focus on in each domain. No one can do everything in the limited time available to us, so it's important to learn to say 'no' to avoid being overcommitted. Overcommitment leads to stress and other issues. So, effective use of time requires us to focus on the most important things in life. When you know your most important and inspiring goals, you can invest most of your time in them without being influenced by distractions. Breaking these goals into smaller, actionable tasks adds clarity and direction.

To more effectively use your time, you should review how you currently use it on a daily or weekly basis and review your accomplishments. Assess your level of satisfaction with the use of your time, and if your level of satisfaction is low, resolve to do something about it. Figure out what the main distractions are that lead you to waste your time. Some common ones include social media, unnecessary meetings, doing unimportant things and interruptions. In terms of social media, it is often best to turn off notifications and work in a quiet space.

Creating a daily to-do list also helps in using time effectively. When you keep that list in front of you, it enhances your focus on the tasks, and this increases productivity and happiness. You may also try to assign fixed time periods for different tasks to enhance your accomplishments.

---

84   Folk & Dunn, 2014
85   Aeon, Faber & Panaccio, 2021

Without this, activities tend to expand to fit the space available, which leads to time being wasted. Various apps and calendars can help you to manage your productivity.

Personal vignette

For me, effective use of time happens when I am focused on a single task and determined to complete it on time. Keeping my phone away also helps me to accomplish what I want to get done. But I think the most important factor in my own time management is being clear about what is and isn't important, along with taking care of myself through rest and exercise. This clarity motivates me to invest my time in the most important things in life.

A brief activity for cultivating time

Make a list of the most important areas of your life. Write down the most important activities and tasks related to each one. Then write down the unimportant activities/distractions on which you often spend your time. Write down how you can reduce the time spent on these unimportant activities and distractions. Share your understanding from this exercise with friend or colleague and listen to their feedback. Do this weekly; review your progress after four weeks and make adjustments to more effectively manage your time.

Reflective questions

1. What unpleasant tasks can you reduce to enhance your happiness?
2. Which tasks and activities give you the most happiness and satisfaction?
3. How can you increase your focus on the activities which boost your happiness?
4. What is the relationship between time use and happiness, in your opinion?
5. What would your happiest week look like if you could design your schedule from scratch?
6. What did you learn from Catherine's story?

References and further reading

Aeon, B., Faber, A., & Panaccio, A. (2021) Does time management work? A meta-analysis. *PloS one*, 16(1), e0245066.

Boniwell, I., & Osin, E. (2015) Beyond time management: time use, performance and well-being. *Organizational Psychology*, 5(3), 85-104.

Burt, C. D. B., Weststrate, A., Brown, C., & Champion, F. (2010) Development of the time management environment (TiME) scale. *Journal of Managerial Psychology*, 25(6):649–68.

Claessens, B., van Eerde, W., Rutte, C., and Roe, R. (2007) A review of the time management literature. *Person. Rev.* 36, 255–276. doi: 10.1108/ 00483480710726136

Csikszentmihalyi, M. (2013) *Flow: The psychology of happiness.* London: Random House.

Folk, D., & Dunn, E. (2024) How can people become happier? A systematic review of preregistered experiments. *Annual Review of Psychology*, 75(1), 467-493.

Kahneman, D. (2011) *Thinking, Fast and Slow.* Farrar, Straus and Giroux.

Thongsri, N., Seksan, J., & Warintarawej, P. (2024). Factors Affecting the Happiness of Learners in Higher Education: Attitude, Grade Point Average, and Time Management. Sustainability, 16(18), 8214.

U

Chapter 21:
Uniqueness

"Be yourself; everyone else is already taken."

Oscar Wilde

In ancient India, there was a mythical bird known as the Chātaka. It had a peculiar trait – a small hole in its beak. Due to this hole, the bird was not able to drink water like all other birds. The moment it started to try, water would leak through the hole. Thus, the bird was able to drink only when it rained. The hole in its beak was, the bird thought, its biggest weakness and a kind of trauma. One day, a sage saw the bird's sadness and said, 'You are not flawed; you are unique. Unlike others, you have the gift of drinking only from the purest source

– the rain from the sky.' Hearing this, the bird's perspective shifted. It no longer saw itself as broken but as special. From that day on, it embraced its uniqueness and never felt sad again.

We all are special, and we all are unique. We have a need to be distinguished. Humanistic psychology emphasizes the idea that we should not compare ourselves with others; instead, we should be attuned with our own specific features and accept ourselves as we are. Uniqueness is a key dimension of personal identity and refers to the private sense of experiencing the self that can only be acknowledged by the individual themselves. According to the humanistic psychologist Carl Rogers, acknowledging oneself as a unique individual is the base for developing a self-determined personality, which refers to taking responsibility for one's choices and decisions.[86] It is nearly impossible to actualize one's potential without appreciating one's uniqueness. Likewise, Abraham Maslow, the psychologist who created the famous 'hierarchy of needs', emphasized that uniqueness is the only source from which self-actualization can be derived.[87]

According to the most recent conceptualization of uniqueness, a sense of uniqueness is a personal inclination to acknowledge oneself as having distinctive features with the feeling of worthiness. It refers to feelings of being somehow different and yet worthy, just by virtue of being who one is, which can be considered a kind of non-contingent self-worth. It stresses a personal consideration of one's unique existence, rather than focusing only on the inclination to feel different from others. Celebrating our own uniqueness and that of others influences and fosters meaningful relationships, and it can lead to better outcomes for everyone.

---

86   Rogers, 1961
87   Maslow, 1954

In this story, Stefan Cantore explains how embracing the uniqueness of both coach and client creates a transformative space where learning, growth and happiness unfold:

In my practice as a business coach, I am often struck by the unique characteristics of my clients. Their personalities and diverse life experiences all combine and enable them to bring to the world a unique perspective. I can recall a physically disabled woman executive whose wheelchair was also her office chair. When our coaching relationship began, I was struck by her determination and focus on life. I wondered if our work together would be hindered by the sense I had of our respective differences. As I reflected on how we related over six meetings, I became aware that my uniqueness, far from being a hindrance, offered a space for engagement and struggle. I was prompted to value my own characteristics and accept that my uniqueness could be of service to her. This was not always easy, always being aware of what might feel like misunderstandings on both sides. And yet, the struggle with uniqueness was the place in which good work of change and transformation was done.

My learning was to value and even rejoice in my own unique characteristics as I listen to them and react in different ways in different coaching relationships. My happiness and satisfaction come from conversations with clients where we together blend insights and create something which is, in itself, quite unique. The intimacy of a coaching conversation, where I have been able to listen to another person, reflect on it for myself and then respond, serves not just the client but me as well! I get a sense of happiness from the creativity that is offered by my uniqueness encountering another unique person. Of course, I am sometimes very puzzled by what emerges. Maybe even fearful. I try and resist the temptation to focus on what I might perceive we have in common, what makes us less unique. Rather, I feel happiest when I walk towards my own unique characteristics and those of the client.

> *It is in these conversational, intimate spaces that unique aspects of my personality and combination of skills offer great potential to know another and to be known well by another. What adds to the joy is when I walk away from such conversations feeling enriched and further developed in the unique characteristics that make me who I am becoming. More than this, though, I sense that the learning is transformative of both of us. Something unique happens when unique individuals commit to be with one another in open conversation. In spaces where uniqueness is embraced so learning and change take place. This is a place of great happiness for me.*

Stefan learned that acknowledging his own uniqueness and that of his clients ultimately helped in his clients' success, and in his own success both as a coach and as an individual.

Uniqueness and happiness

Having a sense of uniqueness is emotionally satisfying for all of us, and it is necessary for our psychological welfare. When we recognize our uniqueness, we pursue activities and endeavours that are aligned with who we are, thereby gaining a strong sense of satisfaction and fulfilment.

In his book *Man's Search for Meaning*, Victor Frankl stated that a sense of personal uniqueness is a basic requirement for finding meaning in life and happiness.[88] A sense of uniqueness is an unconditional self-worth due to being a unique individual rather than any other specific personal features, and it is associated with positive functioning and good mental health. Research has also shown that self-worth is one of the strongest predictors of happiness.[89] A sense of uniqueness provides us a greater freedom to choose our own ways of living rather than being dependent on others and living according to others' expectations.

Scientific evidence

In a research study, Şimşek and Demir argued that a strong personal sense of uniqueness provides individuals with more freedom in their

---

88   Frankl, 1959
89   Lyubomirsky, Tkach & DiMatteo, 2006

choices because they tend to act in accordance with their own emotions, beliefs and thoughts.[90] In another study, uniqueness and happiness were found to be closely related, with authenticity enhancing happiness through the mediating role of feeling unique.[91] A sense of uniqueness provides us with the opportunity to appreciate our true self and thus to minimize the gap between our actions and thoughts.

Empirical research has found that a sense of uniqueness is strongly and positively associated with happiness, as well as other mental health variables such as resilience, dispositional hope and the satisfaction of basic psychological needs, and negatively associated with anxiety and depression.[92] Embracing one's uniqueness aligns with the principles of positive psychology. Following broaden-and-build theory, embracing one's uniqueness can elicit positive emotions.[93] These positive emotions can broaden our cognitive abilities, leading to the development of resources such as social support, resilience, skills and knowledge. These enhanced resources can then help improve health, happiness and fulfilment.

The following flowchart describes the cycle of uniqueness and personal growth:

Discover uniqueness
↓
Embrace uniqueness
↓
Express uniqueness in daily life
↓
Receive positive feedback
↓
Strengthen uniqueness attributes
↓
Experience happiness and self-worth
↓
Discover new aspects of uniqueness
(the cycle repeats)

---

90   Şimşek & Demir, 2014
91   Koydemir *et al.*, 2020
92   Şimşek & Yalınçetin, 2010
93   Fredrickson, 2001

Cultivating uniqueness

Having supportive and intimate exchanges in close relationships has the potential to promote one's sense of uniqueness, which, as discussed, represents a kind of non-contingent self-worth. Spending time with a close friend – collaborating, disclosing personal information to each other, and providing and receiving emotional support – can encourage the development of uniqueness for both parties. A sense of uniqueness can be cultivated by providing positive feedback to others when they talk about their hobbies, their plans for the future and their social relationships by capitalizing on the distinctiveness of their activities and social experiences.

When we have discovered our unique talents, characteristics and strengths, we can invest time and effort in activities aligned to them. This will help in further refining and developing them. We can also seek feedback from others about strengthening our unique talents, such as from mentors, coaches and supportive friends and family members, and we can seek out new opportunities to further enhance our talents, which we can then use to positively impact others.

Personal vignette

My own sense of uniqueness stems from a seamless integration of teaching, coaching, research, writing, training and organizing events – reflecting my passion for learning, sharing and creating. This awareness helps me in making decisions and pursuing my interests. Through my unique attributes, I have developed strong relationships with people in many domains; their feedback strengthens those attributes, along with my resolve to use them more in my life.

A brief activity for cultivating uniqueness

Make a list of your unique attributes. Choose two attributes from the list. Reflect on how you are using those attributes in different areas of your life and identify areas where you could use them more. Explore new opportunities and develop a plan for using them more intentionally. Celebrate the successes you achieve by using your unique attributes – for example, if you believe that good listening is a part of your uniqueness, spend some time helping a friend or colleague by being there for them, or simply listening to them talk. When you have explored both attributes, repeat the cycle with the new set of unique attributes.

Reflective questions

1. Which of your characteristics are unique to you and set you apart from others?

2. How has being yourself has contributed to your happiness?

3. Think of instances when you were not fully yourself. How did it impact your happiness?

4. How effectively do you use your unique attributes in your work, relationships and life?

5. Are there situations or contexts in which you tend to underutilize your unique attributes?

6. What positive outcomes have you achieved from using your uniqueness?

7. When was the last time you took time to reflect on your unique strengths and talents?

8. In which areas of your life would you like to use your unique talents and interests more?

9. What did you learn from Stefan's story?

References and further reading

Frankl, V. E. (1959) *Man's Search for Meaning: An introduction to logotherapy.* Boston: Beacon.

Fredrickson, B. L. (2001) The role of positive emotions in positive psychology: The broaden-and-build theory of positive emotions. *American Psychologist*, 56(3), 218-226.

Koydemir, S., Şimşek, Ö. F., & Demir, M. (2014) Pathways from personality to happiness: Sense of uniqueness as a mediator. *Journal of Humanistic Psychology*, 54(3), 314-335.

Koydemir, S., Şimşek, Ö. F., Kuzgun, T. B., & Schütz, A. (2020) Feeling special, feeling happy: Authenticity mediates the relationship between sense of uniqueness and happiness. *Current Psychology*, 39, 1589-1599.

Lynn, M., & Snyder, C. R. (2002) Uniqueness seeking. In: C. R. Snyder & S. J. Lopez (Eds.), *Handbook of Positive Psychology* (pp395–410). Oxford University Press.

Lyubomirsky, S., Tkach, C., & DiMatteo, M. R. (2006) What are the differences between happiness and self-esteem? *Social Indicators Research*, 78, 363–404.

Maslow, A. H. (1954) *Motivation and Personality.* New York: Harper and Row

O'Neil, I., Ucbasaran, D., & York, J. G. (2022) The evolution of founder identity as an authenticity work process. *Journal of Business Venturing*, 37(1), 106031.

Rogers, C. R. (1961) *On Becoming a Person: A therapist's view of psychotherapy*. London: Constable.

Şimşek, Ö. F., & Demir, M. (2014) A cross-cultural investigation into the relationships among parental support for basic psychological needs, sense of uniqueness, and happiness. *The Journal of Psychology*, 148(4), 387-411.

Şimşek, Ö. F., & Yalınçetin, B. (2010) I feel unique, therefore I am: The development and preliminary validation of the personal sense of uniqueness (PSU) scale. *Personality and Individual Differences*, 49(6), 576-581.

V

Chapter 22:

Values

"True happiness is found in living a life that aligns with our deepest values."

Tony Robbins

Values are the beliefs that guide our behaviour, actions and decisions. Knowing and aligning our values with our actions, decisions, preferences and behaviours contributes to happiness and fulfilment. This is living life according to what matters most to us, and it leads to a sense of authenticity and purpose. Living in alignment with our values involves various areas of life, such as relationships, work, personal development and the use of resources available to us. It requires a deep understanding of one's values, and a commitment to maintain them in daily life. Being aligned with our values helps with positive outcomes across various life domains.

> **Our values guide our lives; yet they can evolve, creating conflict. Ana Paula Nacif shares the story of a successful professional who came to realize his true longings lay elsewhere:**
>
> *Our understanding of our values provides a sense of purpose, direction and fulfilment. They also serve as a compass in our lives, influencing our choices and shaping our goals. Values are a fundamental cornerstone in coaching, and they can have a significant impact on a client's perspective on life and their daily experiences.*
>
> *An example is a client who, at the age of forty, sought coaching for career development. He was highly accomplished and seen by his firm as a high-potential individual. Initially, the focus of the coaching was on reaching the next level in the company. However, as the coaching progressed, it became clear to my client that he no longer had the same drive for career growth that he once had. We did a session on values, and he realized that he was conflicted between values he held at the beginning of his career, which were also aligned with external expectations, mainly from his family and peers, and what was important to him now. He was longing for a meaningful relationship and to explore his passion for writing.*
>
> *He decided to use the coaching to figure out how to make space for the things he truly valued in his life, alongside his demanding career, and to address the challenges his choices posed to both his personal and professional life. As a result, he experienced a renewed sense of purpose and felt happier about his life choices.*

Ana's client's realization transformed his perspective. By exploring his values and realigning his life around them, he found greater fulfilment, balancing career success with personal joy. His journey reminds us that happiness comes not from external expectations, but from honouring what truly matters to us.

Values and happiness

Our values empower us to live authentically, true to ourselves and our beliefs. This authenticity nurtures a deep sense of self-respect and inner peace, contributing to overall happiness. When we prioritize our values in decision making, relationships and the pursuit of our goals, we can experience a deep sense of purpose that contributes to greater well-being and life satisfaction.

Aligning values helps us to foster authentic connections and relationships with other people. Sharing common values creates meaningful connections due to mutual respect, understanding and support. These authentic relationships offer a sense of belonging and connection, which enhances happiness. Living in alignment with one's values encourages personal growth, self-discovery and self-actualization. When we strive to embody our values in various aspects of life, it increases our potential and helps us develop new skills. We cultivate a deeper understanding of ourselves. This ongoing process of growth and development enhances self-esteem, confidence and fulfilment, contributing to happiness.

Scientific evidence

In one study, personal values were found to be an important predictor of happiness.[94] When people live by their values, their lives become more fulfilling and meaningful, leading to a happier existence. Pursuing our values helps to satisfy our need for autonomy, competence and relatedness, leading to higher well-being. A study by Lilach Sagiv, Sonia Roccas and Osnat Hazzan found that values are likely to lead to well-being when they are congruent with the values that prevail in one's social environment.[95] The results of this study also suggested that attainment of values – any values – leads to a positive sense of well-being. Another study conducted by Sonja Lyubomirsky, Kennon Sheldon and David Schkade found that finding new activities that fit one's values enhances happiness.[96]

---

94   Sherman *et al.*, 2021
95   Sagiv, Roccas & Hazan, 2004
96   Lyubomirsky, Sheldon & Schkade, 2005

The following flowchart summarises how living according to one's values is related to happiness:

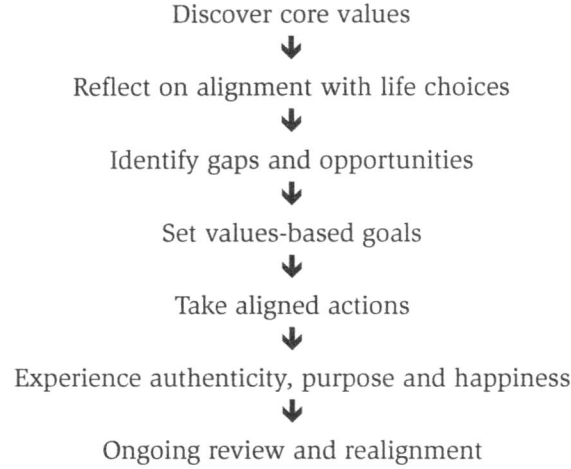

Discover core values
↓
Reflect on alignment with life choices
↓
Identify gaps and opportunities
↓
Set values-based goals
↓
Take aligned actions
↓
Experience authenticity, purpose and happiness
↓
Ongoing review and realignment

Cultivating values

Reflecting on what matters most in life can inspire you to align your behaviours, choices and resources with your core values. Set goals in various aspects of your life that are aligned with your core values, and actively seek opportunities that you feel are value-aligned. Joining groups that work in areas which appeal to you can provide avenues for doing value-aligned activities, projects and tasks, and consciously blocking out time each week can make it easier for you to indulge in some of the most valuable things in your life. As ever, involving friends, family and colleagues can give you a powerful boost in staying focused and prioritizing what really matters.

Personal vignette

One of the most profound ways in which we can cultivate happiness is to discover what truly matters to us – and then to have the courage to shape our lives around it. Whenever I have completed value assessment exercises, I have always found my most important values to be centred around my family. This has directly influenced most of my life decisions, including my choice of job, how I spend my time and other resources, and how I spend my free time.

A brief activity for cultivating values

Sit down in a peaceful spot and spend some time thinking about your most important values. List them, then prioritize them on the basis of their importance to you. Reflect on your recent behaviours and choices, and review how they aligned with your core values. If possible, do this with a trusted friend. Then identify opportunities to better align your behaviours and choices with your core values. Set one or two values-based goals for yourself. Commit to take concrete actions towards these goals and review your progress at regular intervals.

Reflective questions

1. How might living in alignment with your core values contribute to your overall sense of fulfilment and well-being?
2. What obstacles or challenges do you face in living in alignment with your core values?
3. What legacy do you hope to leave behind, based on your values?
4. Which small action can you take this week to better align your life with your core values?
5. What did you learn from Ana's client's story?

References and further reading

De Leon, J. (2024) Conceptualizing Self-Actualization and Self-Fulfillment in the Hispanic/Latiné Individuals Living in America Through the Positive Psychology Theory of Well-Being (Doctoral dissertation, Adler University).

Dolan, S. L. (2020) The secret of coaching and leading by values: Alignment and realignment. In: S. L. Dolan (Ed) *The Secret of Coaching and Leading by Values* (pp. 142-161). Routledge.

Gardner, W. L., Avolio, B. J., Luthans, F., May, D. R., & Walumbwa, F. (2005) 'Can you see the real me?' A self-based model of authentic leader and follower development. *The Leadership Quarterly*, 16(3), 343-372.

Hampton, T. (n.d.) *Living By Your Values and Your Happiness*. Available at: https:// takenyahampton.com/living-by-your-values-and-your-happiness (accessed May 2025).

Hossain, K. A. (2023) Evaluation of ethical values to develop global human resource. *Journal of Liberal Arts and Humanities*, 4(4), 1-29.

Ivtzan, I., Gardner, H. E., Bernard, I., Sekhon, M., & Hart, R. (2013) Wellbeing through self-fulfilment: Examining developmental aspects of self-actualization. *The Humanistic Psychologist*, 41(2), 119-132.

Lu, P., Oh, J., Leahy, K. E., & Chopik, W. J. (2021) Friendship importance around the world: Links to cultural factors, health, and well-being. *Frontiers in Psychology*, 11, 570839.

Lyubomirsky, S., Sheldon, K. M., & Schkade, D. (2005) Pursuing happiness: The architecture of sustainable change. *Review of General Psychology*, 9(2), 111-131.

McGillicuddy, D. (2024) *Educaring from the Heart: How to nurture your wellbeing and re-discover your purpose in education*. Taylor & Francis.

Neiterman, E., & Ladha, R. (2022) Values alignment. In: S. Webber *et al* (Eds), *Understanding and Cultivating Well-being for the Pediatrician: A compilation of the latest evidence in pediatrician well-being science* (pp303-322). Cham: Springer International Publishing.

Rampersad, H. K. (2009) Authentic personal branding: A new blueprint for building and aligning a powerful leadership brand. *IAP*.

Ruslan, N. F. N., Goh, H. C., Hattam, C., Edwards-Jones, A., & Moh, H. H. (2022) Mangrove ecosystem services: Contribution to the well-being of the coastal communities in Klang Islands. *Marine Policy*, 144, 105222.

Ryan, R. M., & Deci, E. L. (2000) Self-determination theory and the facilitation of intrinsic motivation, social development, and well-being. *American Psychologist*, 55(1), 68-78.

Sagiv, L., Roccas, S., Hazan, O. (2004) Value pathways to well-being: Healthy values, valued goal attainment, and environmental congruence. In: P. A. Linley & S. Joseph (Eds.) *Positive Psychology in Practice*. Hoboken, NJ: Wiley.

Sherman, A., Shavit, T., Barokas, G., & Kushnirovich, N. (2021) On the role of personal values and philosophy of life in happiness technology. *Journal of Happiness Studies*, 22, 1055-1070.

Titus-Casseus, M. (2023) *The Art of Inner Peace: A 10-step guide to manifesting your ultimate self*. Money Marv Publishing LLC.

Chapter 23:
Willingness

"Happiness is not something ready-made.
It comes from your own actions."

Dalai Lama

Willingness is an openness and readiness to take steps to enhance our own happiness. We cannot begin to improve our happiness until we are willing to do so. Science has shown that happiness can be increased through well-designed interventions, and both research evidence and everyday experience suggest that actively engaging in the right practices is essential for boosting happiness. A willingness to change one's own happiness and satisfaction levels is the starting point for living a more fulfilling life. Such willingness springs partly from expectations. When we believe that our happiness can be changed, we put in the effort to change it.

> **Willingness opens doors to growth and fulfilment. In this story, Andrea Giraldez-Hayes shows how a willingness to explore, adapt and take risks can shape a meaningful and joyful life:**
>
> *Willingness has always been a subtle undercurrent in my life, although I only recognized it later. Defined by psychologists as being open to change, trying new things and participating in life despite discomfort or fear, willingness began as a natural curiosity and evolved into the foundation of my happiness. Alongside curiosity, love of learning, appreciation of beauty and excellence, perseverance and creativity are my signature character strengths, which have fuelled my willingness. I could share many examples, but I have chosen one.*
>
> *As a descendant of immigrants, I dreamt of exploring the world. At seventeen, I moved to a new country, unfamiliar with the language and without a safety net. Believing that life begins at the edge of one's comfort zone, I discovered the beauty of cultural diversity and my ability to thrive in uncertainty. This pattern continued. At twenty-three, I moved to Barcelona to carry on my music studies. With no job, I nervously joined street performers, an experience that propelled my career. By twenty-nine, another relocation brought professional setbacks, but my openness taught me valuable lessons about vulnerability and self-worth.*

At forty-five, despite being at the top of my career, a position many would consider the height of success, I felt an itch I couldn't ignore. Despite my achievements, title and security, I wanted to pursue a postponed dream. So, I made a choice that baffled my colleagues and even some friends – I pivoted. I changed careers entirely, diving into psychology, a field I was passionate about. It was terrifying, but that same willingness to embrace uncertainty guided me. And it paid off. Not just in terms of professional growth but in a deep, intrinsic sense of happiness I hadn't felt in years. At fifty, I found myself living in yet another new country, with a career that excited me every day and a life that felt authentically my own.

Research indicates that willingness promotes psychological flexibility, a crucial predictor of well-being. By embracing all experiences, we become more resilient and fulfilled. My happiness came not from avoiding discomfort, but from stepping into the unknown with an open heart.

Happiness is not just something we find – it's something we create through our willingness to engage fully with life. Willingness is a force that shapes our happiness. Whether it's trying something new, embracing change or facing uncertainty, the more we say 'yes' to possibilities, the more happiness we invite into our journey.

Willingness and happiness

Willingness serves as a foundation for all our efforts towards enhancing happiness, motivating us to take the first steps in the right direction. Without it, no amount of knowledge about how to enhance happiness will yield results. Willingness prompts us to learn about different ways to enhance happiness through reading, reflecting and exploring with colleagues and friends. It encourages us to assess different interventions and choose which ones suit us best. And it helps us to persevere in staying committed to the actions and interventions we decide upon. It is the driving force that motivates us to take actionable steps towards increasing our happiness, and it shows up in simple daily choices such starting a gratitude journal, going for a morning walk, joining a dance class or calling an old friend. These small steps reflect our willingness – our openness to engage with life and build happiness.

Scientific evidence

Research consistently shows that willingness plays a vital role in enhancing happiness. In a longitudinal study, Lyubomirsky *et al* found that, to become happier, people need both a will and a way.[97] They also suggested that people need to do something that is objectively effective at raising happiness. Therefore, enhancing happiness requires not only willingness to take action but also a means to do so. They further emphasized that the amount of effort that study participants applied to the intervention activities was directly related to improvements in their subsequent happiness. Numerous meta-analysis studies have also supported that positive psychology interventions can be effective in enhancing happiness and well-being.

Cultivating willingness

When we truly believe that happiness can be enhanced, we are much more likely to put in the effort to make it a reality. Encouragement from family and friends to enhance happiness and live a good life increases our willingness to make more effort; similarly, when we hear that happiness is good for our physical and psychological health, we are more likely to take action to enhance it. Understanding the positive impact of higher happiness on career growth, relationships, and overall quality of life all raise our willingness to pursue happiness.

Observing people who actively pursue happiness might motivate you to put in extra effort to increase your own. Join learning events that focus on the idea that happiness is not fixed, and read and discuss evidence-based insights to give you motivation and tools. Understanding the types of activities you engage in and enjoy or find meaningful may also enhance your willingness to put in extra effort towards increasing your happiness. Reflect on what truly matters to you, as this will help

---

97   Lyubomirsky *et al.*, 2011

you align your efforts with your core values. Knowing that your state of mind and happiness affects your loved ones may also motivate you to take action, especially if you wish to get out of a negative state of mind.

Keep things simple to start with – pursue easy, achievable activities for enhancing happiness to help motivate you into action. Before attempting any activity, review whether it is worthwhile, meaningful and/or enjoyable. Explore activities that help in self-expression and fulfilment of potential. People tend to enjoy activities more when they make clear and rapid progress, so simple daily activities are the best way to willingly prioritize your own well-being.

Personal vignette

Trying wholly new things can overwhelming. If you're someone who stresses about anything you start or do, rediscovering past hobbies is a better way to enhance your happiness. Such activities give feelings of nostalgia, and of reliving moments you enjoyed once. And, because the activity is already learned, you can dive straight into enjoyment. For me, reconnecting with my lost inner artist was the best way to manage my stress and increase my happiness.

A brief activity to enhance willingness

Invite colleagues, family members or friends for a discussion about happiness. Ask them to share their views on how happiness can have a positive impact on different areas of life. Once each member has shared their views, invite them to consider how they could be more willing and take more active steps towards enhancing their own happiness. Schedule follow-up discussions on a regular basis to share progress and challenges in the pursuit of happiness.

Reflective questions

1. Identify the types of activities you engage in and enjoy or find meaningful. How can you increase your involvement in those activities?

2. Explore the thoughts and behaviours of happy people you know and consider how that may affect your efforts towards enhancing happiness.

3. How might your willingness to be happy enhance your happiness in general?

4. How has encouragement from others affected your willingness to pursue happiness?

5. How might greater happiness affect different domains of your life?

6. Which activities help you express yourself?

7. What activities might help you to reach your potential?

8. What did you learn from Andrea's story?

References and further reading

Alam, A., & Mohanty, A. (2024) Happiness Engineering: impact of hope-based intervention on life satisfaction, self-worth, mental health, and academic achievement of Indian school students. *Cogent Education*, 11(1), 2341589.

Biggs, A. T., Seech, T. R., Johnston, S. L., & Russell, D. W. (2024) Psychological endurance: How grit, resilience, and related factors contribute to sustained effort despite adversity. *The Journal of General Psychology*, 151(3), 271-313.

Bolier, L., Haverman, M., Westerhof, G. J., Riper, H., Smit, F., & Bohlmeijer, E. (2013) Positive psychology interventions: a meta-analysis of randomized controlled studies. *BMC Public Health*, 13, 1-20.

Gander, F., Proyer, R. T., & Ruch, W. (2016) Positive psychology interventions addressing pleasure, engagement, meaning, positive relationships, and accomplishment increase well-being and ameliorate depressive symptoms: A randomized, placebo-controlled online study. *Frontiers in Psychology*, 7, 686.

Hill, T. G., Coughlan, E. C., & Mackinnon, S. P. (2024) It's the Little Things in Life: Enjoyment of Different Types of Personal Projects. *International Journal of Applied Positive Psychology*, 9(2), 1083-1103.

Lyubomirsky, S., & Layous, K. (2013). How do simple positive activities increase well-being? *Current Directions in Psychological Science*, 22(1), 57-62.

Lyubomirsky, S., Dickerhoof, R., Boehm, J. K., & Sheldon, K. M. (2011) Becoming happier takes both a will and a proper way: an experimental longitudinal intervention to boost well-being. *Emotion*, 11(2), 391.

Lyubomirsky, S., Sheldon, K. M., & Schkade, D. (2005) Pursuing happiness: The architecture of sustainable change. *Review of General Psychology*, 9(2), 111-131.

van Agteren, J., Iasiello, M., Lo, L., Bartholomaeus, J., Kopsaftis, Z., Carey, M., & Kyrios, M. (2021) A systematic review and meta-analysis of psychological interventions to improve mental wellbeing. *Nature Human Behaviour*, 5(5), 631-652.

van den Bogaard, D., Soenens, B., Brenning, K., Flamant, N., & Vansteenkiste, M. (2024) Can students learn to optimize their need-based experiences and mental health during a stressful period? Testing a need-crafting intervention in higher education. *Journal of Happiness Studies*, 25(5), 1-31.

X

Chapter 24:
Xcel

"Progress is not in enhancing what is, but in advancing toward what will be."

Khalil Gibran

Boond-boond se saagar bharta ('drop by drop, the ocean fills') is a timeless Indian saying that highlights the power of small, consistent efforts. Deeply rooted in ancient tradition, it reminds us that a series of small steps can gradually contribute to a much larger outcome. Progress is not always about achieving big milestones, but about small, steady improvements in everyday life. Whether it's learning a new skill, helping someone or becoming more mindful, each step adds value to our journey. These small victories build confidence, foster fulfilment, and together create a sense of growth and purpose. By appreciating and celebrating small achievements, we stay inspired and engaged in our wider pursuit of happiness.

Teresa Amabile and Steven Kramer studied nearly twelve thousand daily diary entries provided by more than two hundred individuals in seven organizations. They published their findings in the book *The Progress Principle: Using small wins to ignite joy, engagement, and creativity at work*.[98] Their research inside organizations revealed that the best way to motivate people, day in and day out, is by facilitating progress – even small wins.

To 'Xcel' (excel) is to progress in small, meaningful actions every day. This is different from achieving highly challenging goals. We all have an innate need to progress in all important domains of life, and excelling is a part of the process by which we try to become better in whatever we attempt. It is improving and sometimes surpassing our own limits. While striving to excel, people gain confidence and a sense of fulfilment. As Richard Boyatzis, Melvin Smith and Ellen van Oosten highlight in their book *Helping People Change*, real growth happens when we align with our deeper motivations, allowing us to excel in ways that are personally meaningful and fulfilling.[99] Moving forward in life irrespective of the pace, ensures that we remain engaged, inspired and hopeful.

---

98 Amabile & Kramer, 2011
99 Boyatzis, Smith & Van Oosten, 2019

Amit Agnihotri's journey from young media professional to pioneering entrepreneur exemplifies how consistent efforts, driven by inner purpose, can create a lasting impact:

My first bold step came in 2000, when I co-founded Exchange4media Group, India's first media and advertising news platform. Eight years later, with just two team members and a small apartment as an office, I launched MBAUniverse.com, an education portal that would go on to guide over a million MBA aspirants. This start-small, click-by-click approach reflects what is known as the 'Kaizen mindset' of continuous improvement. Early on I learnt that if you move in the right direction, each step, however modest, adds to a larger, impactful vision.

In 2010, I created the Indian Management Conclave (IMC) — today India's most respected MBA education conference. IMC has been co-hosted by highly respected Indian business schools and has influenced their policy, pedagogy and leadership development. My mantra is: Focus on impact, not just size.

What keeps me going? A belief that work equals happiness. To me, joy lies not in titles or glory, but in the daily pursuit of meaningful goals. Tired? Often. Unhappy? Never. I live by an inner compass, staying grounded, ignoring the noise, and focusing on what truly matters.

Whether it's guiding students, organizing conferences for course Directors or researching gaps in management education, I continue to make consistent, value-driven progress in shaping management education. My journey shows that fulfillment comes not from sudden leaps, but from continuous, mindful steps toward a purpose-driven life.

In a world chasing overnight success, Amit's story is a powerful reminder that greatness is built not in bursts, but through steady, purposeful progress. It also reinforces that excellence is not about competing with others, but about improving oneself – one click at a time!

Xcel and happiness

Steady, incremental improvements bring us joy and enhance our happiness. Progress fuels a sense of accomplishment and engagement.

Progressing and growing in meaningful activities increases our sense of hope and optimism. Consistency in doing things that we consider important increases our feelings of life satisfaction and reduces the anxiety we may feel when we are not making any effort to move forward. Accomplishments, whether large or small, motivate us to pursue our goals, as well as enhancing self-esteem and reinforcing a growth mindset. This cycle of achievement and reinforcement enhances overall well-being and happiness.

Scientific evidence

Excelling enhances the likelihood of our entering into flow states, helping us have a deep sense of engagement and happiness. According to Bandura's theory of self-efficacy, persistent effort gives us a sense of mastery that contributes to goal achievement and happiness.[100] Consistent effort may also lead to fulfilment of the need for competency, autonomy and relatedness, leading to promotion of well-being. Satisfying these psychological needs enhances happiness. Studies have shown that the intention to excel is perceived as a personal growth initiative which contributes to happiness – in a recent meta-analysis, it was found that personal growth initiative was positively correlated with happiness, self-esteem and self-efficacy.[101]

Cultivating Xcel

To excel, we need to adopt a growth mindset. Knowing and understanding that we can become better in whatever we do can help us to excel in those endeavours. When we see failure as an opportunity to learn, we will keep making efforts to grow. Knowing our interests and passions also help us to become better in those interests and passions, and gives us a boost of energy and inspiration to do more in those areas – we are more inspired to take action, and we feel less tired or exhausted when we do. This persistence, in turn, helps us to progress and excel in those areas, and gives us more wins to celebrate and drive us on.

---

100 Bandura, 1997
101 Jiao, Chen & Lyu, 2024

Personal vignette

Over the past few months, I have been trying to excel in my yoga routine. Achieving better postures with the rhythm of breath always fills me with great satisfaction and happiness. I consider this to be a lifelong journey, and I will continue trying to excel in this area – one small step at a time. The other area in which I want to excel is with my writing projects. Maintaining consistency in this work is always fulfilling, and it spurs me on to new projects and experiences.

A brief activity to enhance Xcel

Invite a group of friends or colleagues to volunteer for this activity. Ask everyone to recall some recent progress they have made in any domain of life. Ask them to describe how they felt before, during and after that progress was made. Facilitate a discussion on how making progress in different areas of life enhances happiness. Ask the participants to share how excelling in those moments inspired them to take other positive steps in their lives.

Reflective questions

1. In which domains of your life might excelling make your life more fulfilling and satisfying?
2. How might excelling in some of your key areas make other people's life better?
3. Which people might motivate you to excel, and how will you enrol them to motivate you?
4. How might celebrating small successes help you to excel?
5. Reflect on the level of satisfaction of excelling in the most important domains of your life.
6. In which domain of your life would you like to implement learning from the 'drop by drop' saying that opened the chapter?
7. What did you learn from Amit's story.

References and further reading

Amabile, T., & Kramer, S. (2011) *The Progress Principle: Using small wins to ignite joy, engagement, and creativity at work*. Harvard Business Press.

Bandura, A. (1997) *Self-efficacy: The exercise of control*. W.H. Freeman and Company.

Bandura, A. (2023) Cultivate self-efficacy for personal and organizational effectiveness. In E. A. Locke & C. L. Cooper (Eds.) *Principles of Organizational Behavior: The handbook of evidence-based management* (3rd ed., pp. 113–135). Wiley.

Boyatzis, R. E., Smith, E., & Van Oosten, E. (2019) *Helping People Change: Coaching with compassion for lifelong learning and growth*. Harvard Business Press.

Csikszentmihalyi, M. (1990) *Flow: The psychology of optimal experience*. Harper & Row.

Deci, E. L., & Ryan, R. M. (2000). The 'what' and 'why' of goal pursuits: Human needs and the self-determination of behavior. *Psychological Inquiry*, 11(4), 227-268.

Jiao, Z., Chen, Y., & Lyu, C. (2024) Factors correlated with personal growth initiative among college students: A meta-analysis. *Heliyon*, 10(7).

Orlick, T. (2015) *In Pursuit of Excellence* (5th ed.). Human Kinetics.

Rhew, E., Piro, J. S., Goolkasian, P., & Cosentino, P. (2018) The effects of a growth mindset on self-efficacy and motivation. *Cogent Education*, 5(1), 1492337.

Sheldon, K. M., & Elliot, A. J. (1999) Goal striving, need satisfaction, and longitudinal well-being: the self-concordance model. *Journal of Personality and Social Psychology*, 76(3), 482-497.

Sheldon, K. M., & Kasser, T. (1998) Pursuing personal goals: Skills enable progress, but not all progress is beneficial. *Personality and Social Psychology Bulletin*, 24(12), 1319-1331.

Y

Chapter 25:

Yay!

"Joy is what happens when we allow ourselves to recognize how good things really are."

Marianne Williamson

Reflect on this statement: *'Yay!' is the language of joy, and happiness is its faithful companion.*

'Yay!' is an informal expression used to express joy, delight, victory or a sense of accomplishment. It is delivered with enthusiasm, and, when written, it is expressed with an exclamation mark. Sometimes people engage in clapping, jumping or other gestures while saying it.

'Yay!' can be much more expressive of joy than simply saying 'I am happy.' The tone of its usage may vary across different situations, for instance when receiving a gift versus overcoming a fear, but 'Yay!' – along with similar expressions such as 'Woohoo!' and 'Hooray!' – always serves to give our spoken communication vitality and rhythm, and to make our communication animated. As such, it forms a subtle but powerful part of our communication.

> **Happiness grows when we express it. In this story, Ekta Singh shares how 'Yay!' not only reflects her joy but also amplifies it, making each reunion with her husband even more special.**
>
> *It's been nine years of marriage, but some things never change. My husband, KK, works on an oil rig, which means he is away for half the month. I am used to the routine – his absence, the silence of the house, the phone calls – but the excitement of his return never fades. Each time he lands in New Delhi, I receive the same text: 'Landed'. And my fingers, almost by instinct, type back: 'Yay!' It's a simple word, just three letters, but for me, it holds the weight of pure joy. In my mind, it's not just a word – it's a feeling. It's the mental picture of my widest smile, the sheer delight bubbling within, the imaginary happy dance I do whenever I know he's home.*
>
> *In many ways, 'Yay!' feels like 'my' word – an extension of my happiness, a verbal expression of a joyful leap. It reminds me of that little child inside me, the one who finds happiness in the smallest of things. A surprise dessert, an unexpected day off, or a sudden breeze on a hot day – each one deserving of a 'Yay!'. But seeing your loved one after a long separation? That can never be a small reason to be happy. If anything, it's the biggest. And that's why no other word fits quite like 'Yay!' to express the pure elation of knowing KK is back.*

Now, KK was never one for expressive texts. His messages were always to the point – no emojis, no extra words, just information. But something changed over time. Maybe happiness really is contagious. One evening, after months of our usual exchange, I sent my enthusiastic 'Yay!' as soon as he texted me. And for the first time, instead of a simple 'Ok' or 'See you soon', I saw his response: 'Yay!' I blinked at my screen, half-smiling, half-surprised. Had he really typed that? The reserved, no-nonsense man I married had just mirrored my excitement? I couldn't help but laugh. Maybe my 'Yay!' had found a way into his heart, just as his presence had always filled mine.

And now, every time I see that word pop up on my screen, I picture him smiling too, miles away but already home in spirit. 'Yay!', indeed.

Expressing joy doesn't just reflect happiness, it amplifies it. Ekta's story reminds us that the act of expressing excitement deepens our happiness and spreads it to those we love. As Ekta beautifully shares, her simple 'Yay!' not only captures her excitement but also intensifies it. When we express our joy freely and openly, we don't just feel happier – we invite others to share in that happiness, making it even more meaningful.

'Yay!' and happiness

'Yay!' is a light-hearted, informal expression of joy that leads to greater well-being. When people express emotion verbally, it becomes more tangible and real. This more tangible emotion may then be savoured, leading to enhanced happiness. When 'Yay!' is expressed, it gives us a sense of elation in our feelings – and, as emotions are contagious, it also affects the moods of other people, enhancing everyone's happiness. Smiling, jumping and clapping while expressing 'Yay!' intensifies happiness. 'Yay!' moments can shift an individual's mental state toward a more positive outlook, helping them to become habitual in finding joy in little things.

Scientific evidence

According to broaden-and-build theory, positive emotions broaden one's cognitive abilities and that broadening builds resources such as social support, resilience, knowledge and skills.[102] These resources enhance happiness, health and fulfilment. Expressing 'Yay!' adds to positive emotions and, using the above rationale, it adds to enhanced overall happiness. Facial feedback hypothesis suggests that having a positive facial expression can influence emotional experience.[103] While expressing 'Yay!' and the facial expressions that accompany it, the brain may read those expressions and intensify the feeling of positive emotion, leading to enhanced feelings of happiness. Expressing happiness through 'Yay!', smiling, or laughing can spread happiness to others through emotional contagion.

Cultivating 'Yay!'

Actively seek and recognize moments of joy and achievement. Sharing moments of joy with others may enhance your happiness and encourage them to share their own 'Yay!' moments, enhancing overall happiness for everyone. Celebrating the successes and accomplishments of other people also builds positive relationships with them, enhancing psychological well-being.

Maintaining a gratitude journal and regularly acknowledging positive moments can enhance opportunities for 'Yay!' expressions. Assigning some time to reflect on what happened during a day can make it easier to spot any 'Yay!' moments that occurred. Savouring past achievements may also refresh memories of 'Yay!' moments, thereby enhancing happiness.

102 Fredrickson, 2001
103 Strack, Martin & Stepper, 1988

Happiness thrives when it is shared – one 'Yay!' at a time. So, follow the 'Yay!' manifesto:

Celebrate small wins

No achievement is too small for a *Yay*! Whether it's finishing a task, enjoying a sunset, or sticking to your daily routine – acknowledge it with a joyful *Yay!*

Express freely

Let your joy be seen, heard and felt. Smile wider, clap louder, jump higher – let your 'Yay!' fill the moment without holding back.

Amplify the joy of others

Cheer for others' victories as if they were your own. Every time you celebrate someone's success, happiness multiplies.

Find 'Yays!' in everyday life

Spot joy in ordinary moments – a hot cup of tea, a kind word, or a playful moment with loved ones. Tiny 'Yays!' create lasting happiness.

Create 'Yay!' rituals

Start the day with a positive affirmation, end it by reflecting on 'Yay!' moments, or share your daily 'Yays!' with friends and family.

Be the source of 'Yay!'

Surprise someone with a small gesture. Encourage, appreciate and uplift others – become a spark of happiness wherever you go.

Personal vignette

'Yay!' has become a part of celebrating success many cultures. Young and old alike use 'Yay!', or similar words, to express unbridled joy. My daughter always expresses happiness by saying 'Yay!' whenever her mother prepares something special for her. She also shouts it whenever she wins in any games we play as a family. I also express my happiness this way when I win games with my family; regrettably, my chances of winning are much lower than hers.

A brief activity for cultivating 'Yay!'

Observe people around you who express their happiness, joy and accomplishment by saying 'Yay!'. Make a list of your previous achievements or positive good behaviours, and sense how that act of recollection affects your facial expressions and other body gestures. For two weeks, at the end of each day, take a few moments to spot 'Yay!' moments that have occurred. Make a small group of friends who will all share their 'Yay!' moments together.

Reflective questions

1. Which activities for you generally produce 'Yay!' expressions accompanied by clapping, jumping, or smiling?

2. How frequently do you express happiness, achievement or gratitude through saying 'Yay!' or similar expressions?

3. How can you create more 'Yay!' moments in your everyday life?

4. How are 'Yay!' moments and happiness related?

5. Observe people who express their joy through 'Yay!' or similar paralinguistic words. What can you learn from those people about happiness?

6. Who are the people in your life whose expressions of happiness inspire your own joy?

7. What did you learn from Ekta's story?

References and further reading

Al Hashimi, S. (2007) Paralinguistic vocal control of interactive media: how untapped elements of voice might enhance the role of non-speech voice input in the user's experience of multimedia (Doctoral dissertation, Middlesex University).

Cameron, G. (2022) Positive emotions are contagious. *Institute of Positive Education*. Available at: https://instituteofpositiveeducation.com/blogs/institute-blog/positive-emotions-are-contagious (accessed May 2025).

Cerretani, J. (2011) The contagion of happiness: Harvard researchers are discovering how we can all get happy. *Harvard Medicine Magazine*, Summer 2011, *The Science of Emotion* Issue. Available at: https://magazine.hms.harvard.edu/science-emotion (accessed May 2025).

Dash, B., & Davis, K. (2022) Significance of nonverbal communication and paralinguistic features in communication: A critical analysis. *International Journal for Innovative Research in Multidisciplinary Field*, 8(4), 172-179.

Fredrickson, B. L. (2001) The role of positive emotions in positive psychology: The broaden-and-build theory of positive emotions. *American Psychologist*, 56(3), 218-226.

Harada, T., Hayashi, A., Sadato, N., & Iidaka, T. (2016) Neural correlates of emotional contagion induced by happy and sad expressions. *Journal of Psychophysiology*.

Jacobson, C., Hill, R. M., Pettit, J. W., & Miranda, R. (2015) The Measure of Verbally Expressed Emotion: Development and factor structure of a scale designed to assess comfort expressing feelings to others. *Journal of Psychopathology and Behavioral Assessment*, 37(2), 358–369.

Kataria, M. (2020) *Laughter Yoga: Daily laughter practices for health and happiness*. Hachette UK.

Lee, Y. (2024) From an affirmative response to a discourse marker: Focusing on the Korean interjection ney (Doctoral dissertation, UCLA).

Lin, D., Zhu, T., & Wang, Y. (2024) Emotion contagion and physiological synchrony: The more intimate relationships, the more contagion of positive emotions. *Physiology & Behavior*, 275, 114434.

Schulz, J. (2017) Emotions are contagious: Learn what science and research has to say about it. *Michigan State University Extension*. Available at: www.canr.msu.edu (accessed May 2025).

Strack, F., Martin, L. L., & Stepper, S. (1988) Inhibiting and facilitating conditions of the human smile: a nonobtrusive test of the facial feedback hypothesis. *Journal of Personality and Social Psychology*, 54(5), 768.

Tielman, M., Neerincx, M., Meyer, J. J., & Looije, R. (2014) Adaptive emotional expression in robot-child interaction. In: *Proceedings of the 2014 ACM/IEEE international conference on Human-robot interaction* (pp. 407-414).

Wong, E., & Tschan, F. (2013) Expressing and amplifying positive emotions facilitate goal attainment in workplace interactions. *Frontiers in Psychology*, 4, 188.

Бащенко, В. В. (2023) *Interjections in Modern English Dialogical Discourse: A study of movie scripts*.

Z

Chapter 26:

Zest

"Don't ask what the world needs. Ask what makes you come alive, and go do it. Because what the world needs is people who have come alive."

Howard Thurman

Zest is the ability to approach life with excitement and energy. Individuals with zest are full of spirit and participate fully and actively in everything they do. Zest is not just an attitude; it's a way of life. It transforms the ordinary into the extraordinary and the routine into adventure. When we embrace zest, we don't just seek happiness – we infuse happiness into every moment.

Zest is one of the character strengths within the Virtues in Action (VIA) Classification of Virtues and Strengths given by Chris Peterson and Martin Seligman.[104] They classify zest as 'vitality, enthusiasm, vigor, energy, approaching life with excitement and energy; not doing things halfway or half-heartedly; living life as an adventure; feeling alive and activated.' People with zest exhibit high levels of energy and enjoy life a lot. They seek out and appreciate the joys both large and small that life has to offer. They are always eager to explore new places, ideas and experiences. They can find joy even in routine tasks. They immerse themselves fully in activities, and they inspire others with their enthusiasm and energy.

Zest and happiness

Individuals with zest are often more engaged and motivated, and they are likely to find fulfilment in their endeavours. As they are fully immersed in whatever activities they are doing, this often leads to a state of 'flow', helping to reduce stress and increase happiness. They find interest and joy even in routine tasks and turn mundane activities into enjoyable ones. Due to their infectious energy, they boost enthusiasm and energy in other people. They approach life with spirit and verve, which buffers against stress and other negative emotions, and, due to their positive outlook, they perceive and maximize joy in everyday situations.

Zest enhances resilience and fulfilling relationships, leading to greater happiness and satisfaction. Due to an overall active approach to life, individuals with zest enjoy better physical health, which in turn leads to enhanced mental health and happiness. When we approach life with excitement and curiosity, even ordinary moments become extraordinary. Zest is about embracing experiences with eagerness, passion and a sense of adventure. Happiness often thrives on energy, enthusiasm and engagement – the very qualities that define zest.

---

104 Peterson & Seligman, 2004

One of the best ways to witness zest in action is through the joy of planning and experiencing something new. Consider this story from Santoshi Sengupta:

It is a bright sunny day. My university has declared vacation for us. My kids' school has declared vacation for them. And my husband has declared a few days off from his work. All four of us work out a common slot of four to five days and that sets the ground for our short family trip aiming at exploring our country, its unity in diversity, its culture and cuisine, its flora and fauna, and its people and practices. We choose a state, plan out an itinerary covering the important (and sometimes, not so important) destinations, book our tickets and accommodation, and with this, we, especially I, step into a whole new world of enthusiasm.

Travelling makes my heart jump with leaps and bounds, and more than the actual travel, it is the planning that makes me more elated and give wings to my imagination. With a zest for new experiences, we make travel plans that bring us pure happiness and unforgettable memories. The anticipation of the trip with my husband and children to a new place in our vibrant colourful India creates a sense of happiness and hopefulness. Connecting with others, discussing the itinerary, packing our stuff lifts my mood and teleports my mind and focus from the daily mundane life to a new exciting expedition. This enthusiasm creates a positive mindset, enhances my engagement levels, and triggers happy hormones. I can feel that in myself as I start singing upbeat songs, start sprinting rhythmically, interact positively and happily with others, and visualize moments in the trip cuddling with my family.

These travel plans, which are fuelled by zest, bring me unmatched happiness with every new destination we explore. Such travel enthusiasm is a perfectly positive feeling, which shapes the mind and the outlook in a constructive way that brings more meaning to my life, widens my perspective, and gives an opportunity to connect with humankind at a much deeper level.

Santoshi's enthusiasm for her upcoming trip transformed her mindset and filled her with happiness. Her story beautifully illustrates how zest fuels happiness – not just in the actual experience, but also in the anticipation, planning, and engagement. Santoshi's zest not only uplifts her own happiness but also spreads contagious positivity to her family, creating shared moments of joy. Whether it's travel, learning or pursuing a new challenge, an enthusiastic approach expands our perspectives, deepens our connections and elevates our joy.

Scientific evidence

Research studies have shown that zest is a good predictor of subjective well-being. In a study involving a sample of more than five thousand participants, it was found that zest was robustly related to life satisfaction.[105] In a recent study, zest was found to be strongly related to happiness, well-being and resilience.[106] Individuals with zest are often internally motivated and do things for their own sake rather than for external rewards. Research has supported the strong association of zest with satisfying the need for autonomy, competence and relatedness.[107] Following self-determination theory, these individuals may feel happier as the activities they pursue are aligned with their values and interests.[108]

Individuals with zest approach tasks with excitement and energy, and they are more likely to have flow experiences more often, contributing to happiness and fulfilment. Broaden-and-build theory suggests that positive emotions such as zest and joy enhance cognitive abilities and resources such as skills, social support for individuals leading to enhanced happiness.[109] Research has also supported that zest precludes boredom and anxiety.[110]

Cultivating zest

Identify activities that energize and excite you. Working on personally meaningful goals may increase zest and motivation to achieve those goals. Seeking out new experiences and challenges leads to greater zest,

105 Park, Peterson & Seligman, 2004
106 Karris Bachik, Carey & Craighead, 2021
107 Brdar & Kashdan, 2010
108 Ryan & Deci, 2000
109 Fredrickson, 2001
110 Peterson & Seligman, 2004

and engaging regularly in physical activities may boost energy levels and enhance a positive mood. Working in groups can also nurture zest for many individuals. Surround yourself with people who encourage and energize you to exert a high level of effort, and look for the joy in everyday moments. Maintain a hopeful attitude by generating different pathways to reach a goal. Zest may also emerge by acknowledging one's role in a particular context needing energy and enthusiasm. Observe people with zest, and try to understand what the reasons might be behind their high levels of energy and excitement.

Whenever possible, try to follow the following rules for living with zest:

Live with energy, not just existence

Seek joy in both the grand adventures and the tiny moments

Approach life with curiosity and courage

Inspire others by bringing your full self to every task

Celebrate your victories, big or small

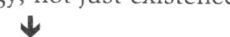

Never lose the spark to explore, learn and play

Personal vignette

I can well remember organizing my very first international conference. My excitement was palpable – from preparing materials to imagining the myriad conversations that would unfold during the course of the event. This infectious energy not only lifted my own mood but also inspired others to participate actively. That experience, and many others since, taught me the important lesson that enthusiasm is often more contagious than knowledge.

A brief activity for developing zest

Write down three to five activities from your childhood that you used to undertake with great excitement and energy. From those activities, set a challenging goal for the next week in an area of your interest. Engage yourself in that activity. If you can't think of a childhood activity to pursue now, you could also use art, music and writing to explore your creative side. Celebrate your success after achieving your goal or making substantial progress towards it.

Reflective questions

1. What activities would you like to do that excite and energize you?
2. With whom do you generally feel inspired and energized?
3. How might zest help you to enhance your happiness and life satisfaction?
4. What generally makes people high in energy and excitement?
5. How might hope and confidence help you nurture zest?
6. What can you learn from children showing enthusiasm towards whatever they do?
7. Think of a situation in which you used zest. How did it help you in that situation?
8. What did you learn from Santoshi's story?

References and further reading

Aytaç, A., Şahin, Ç., Görgülü, D., Dilber, Y., & Direk, A. (2024) The relationship between teachers' zest for work and teaching motivation: the mediating role of achievement goals. *Frontiers in Psychology*, 15, 1362920.

Brdar, I., & Kashdan, T. (2010) Character strengths and well-being in Croatia. *Journal of Research in Personality*, 44, 151–154.

Buschor, C., Proyer, R. T., & Ruch, W. (2013) Self- and peer-rated character strengths: How do they relate to satisfaction with life and orientations to happiness? *Journal of Positive Psychology*, 8, 116–127.

Csikszentmihalyi, M. (2002) *Flow: The classic work on how to achieve happiness*. Rider.

Fredrickson, B. L. (2001) The role of positive emotions in positive psychology: The broaden-and-build theory of positive emotions. *American Psychologist*, 56(3), 218-226.

Gajdošová, E., Petrulytė, A., & Svence, G. (2022) Resilience and Social Emotional Health of Teachers in Slovakia, Latvia, Lithuania in Pandemic Times. *Psychology*, 12(7), 425-443.

Glasberg, A. L., Pellfolk, T., & Fagerström, L. (2014) Zest for life among 65-and 75-year-olds in Northern Finland and Sweden–a cross-sectional study. *Scandinavian Journal of Caring Sciences*, 28(2), 328-336.

Karris Bachik, M. A., Carey, G., & Craighead, W. E. (2021) VIA character strengths among US college students and their associations with happiness, well-being, resiliency, academic success and psychopathology. *The Journal of Positive Psychology*, 16(4), 512-525.

Lam, K. K. L. (2021) The mediating effect of gratitude in the relationship between zest for life and depression. *Personality and Individual Differences*, 171, 110476.

Lapierre, S., Chauvette, S., Bolduc, L., Adams-Lemieux, M., Boller, B., & Desjardins, S. (2023) Character strengths and resilience in older adults during the COVID-19 pandemic. *Canadian Journal on Aging/La Revue canadienne du vieillissement*, 42(3), 455-465.

Niemiec, R. M. (2022) The strengths-based workbook for stress relief: A character strengths approach to finding calm in the chaos of daily life. MJ Family Services. Available at: www. mjfamilyservices.ca/home/wp-content/uploads/2022/05/The-Strengths-Based-Workbook-for-Stress-Relief_-A-Character-Strengths-Approach-to-Finding-Calm-in-the-Chaos-of-Daily-Life-PDFDrive-.pdf (accessed May 2025).

Park, N., Peterson, C., & Seligman, M. E. (2004) Strengths of character and well-being. *Journal of social and Clinical Psychology*, 23(5), 603-619.

Peterson, C., & Seligman, M. E. P. (2004) *Character Strengths and Virtues: A handbook and classification*. Oxford University Press.

Peterson, C., Park, N., Hall, N., & Seligman, M. E. (2009) Zest and work. *Journal of Organizational Behavior: The International Journal of Industrial, Occupational and Organizational Psychology and Behavior*, 30(2), 161-172.

Peterson, C., Ruch, W., Beermann, U., Park, N., & Seligman, M. E. (2007) Strengths of character, orientations to happiness, and life satisfaction. *The Journal Of Positive Psychology*, 2(3), 149-156.

Rashid, T., Summers, R.F., Seligman, M.E.P. (2024) Positive Psychology Model of Mental Function and Behavior. In: Tasman, A., et al. Tasman's Psychiatry (pp. 1055–1078). Springer, Cham.

Ryan, R. M., & Deci, E. L. (2000) Self-determination theory and the facilitation of intrinsic motivation, social development, and well-being. *American Psychologist*, 55(1), 68-78.

Spreitzer, G., Porath, C. L., & Gibson, C. B. (2012) Toward human sustainability: How to enable more thriving at work. *Organizational Dynamics*, 41(2), 155-162.

Conclusion

Now that you've read *Happiness A-Z*, I hope it has been an inspiring journey. This book is intended to be not just a one-time read, but a resource you can revisit whenever you want to boost your happiness. Keep reflecting on what you've learned, and keep applying these insights in your daily life.

Happiness is a habit—one that can be cultivated through consistent effort. While high achievements contribute to happiness, true and lasting happiness comes from practicing evidence-based strategies. Each chapter in this book has presented compelling scientific evidence showing how different attitudes and actions are closely linked to happiness. By consciously developing these attitudes, you can enhance your well-being in meaningful ways.

At any given moment, we can identify the strategy that best suits our needs. Being able to choose the right approach for different situations makes happiness more accessible and sustainable. Some strategies are even more powerful when practiced alongside others – while peer learning and shared experiences amplify their impact. Revisiting the reflective questions in each chapter will help you stay engaged with your happiness journey.

I encourage you to share the insights from *Happiness A-Z* with others. By doing so, you are not only strengthening your own happiness but also helping to create ripples of joy in the lives of those around you. Imagine a world where happiness is contagious, where each of us actively contributes to a kinder, more fulfilled society. Together, we can make this vision a reality.

Thank you for being part of this journey. Your commitment to happiness – both for yourself and for others – is truly inspiring. Keep growing, keep sharing, and keep spreading happiness!